THE POWER OF KNOW

IN THE

WORD — WORKS — WORSHIP

HERSTINE WRIGHT

SONFLOWER
PUBLISHING
© Chicago, Illinois

THE POWER OF KNOW by Herstine Wright

SONFLOWER PUBLISHING™
P.O. Box 439468
Chicago, IL 60643

Copyright ©2020 by Herstine Wright
All Rights Reserved

Library of Congress Catalog Card Number 2020917747

According to the 1976 United States Copyright Act, no part of this book may be reproduced or transmitted in any form or by any means, electronic, mechanical, photocopying, recording, or otherwise for commercial gain or profit without written permission from the publisher. The use of short quotations or occasional page copying for personal group study is permitted and encouraged. Permission will be granted upon request. Unless otherwise identified, Scripture quotations are from the King James and Revised Standard Versions of the Bible. Emphasis within Scripture is the author's own. Please note that Sonflower's publishing style capitalizes certain pronouns in Scripture that refer to the Father, Son, and Holy Spirit, and may differ from some Bible publishers' styles.

Take note that the name satan and related names are not capitalized. We choose not to acknowledge him under any circumstance.

ISBN 978-0-9887797-6-1
For Worldwide Distribution
Printed and Bound in the
United States of America

For more information on where to purchase this and the release of future Sonflower Publishing Books
reach us on the internet:
http://www.sonflowerpublishing.com
sonflowerpublishing1@gmail.com
writeher1@juno.com

CONTENTS

Prayers
Acknowledgements
Introduction
THE POWER OF *KNOW*

PART I
For *Purpose*

CHAPTER 1	*Mankind's* Purpose	3
CHAPTER 2	*Appearance*	7
CHAPTER 3	*Preservation*	11
CHAPTER 4	*'Fully'*	15
CHAPTER 5	*'Called'*	23

PART II
In The *Word*

CHAPTER 6	*Empowered* or *Overpowered*?	31
CHAPTER 7	If Demons *KNOW*, Why Don't The Believers?	37
CHAPTER 8	The *Author* and *Teacher* Inside	43
CHAPTER 9	*'Tell'* and *'Show'*	51
CHAPTER 10	The *'Tell'* of Two Voices	55

PART III
In The *Worship*

CHAPTER 11	The *'Tell'* of Two *'Wells'*...	67
CHAPTER 12	*Hail!* Prevails Against Hell..	73
CHAPTER 13	*Never Again!* The *Aroma* That *Erases*..........................	79
CHAPTER 14	*Knowledge of* His Glory..	83

PART IV
In The *Works*

CHAPTER 15	*FIRST* Works..	97
CHAPTER 16	*Performing* the *Exploits*...	103
CHAPTER 17	*Be* Ready and *Keep* Ready...	111
CHAPTER 18	*Zealous*	115
CHAPTER 19	*Abiding Fruit*..	121
CHAPTER 20	*STAR* Power or Star-Struck?..	127
CHAPTER 21	The *Fear* of the LORD—A *Strategy* to *Persuade*.......	131
CHAPTER 22	*Rewards* —What's Your Credit Score?............................	139
Summary...		151

PRAYER OF THANKSGIVING

Father, I thank You for being LORD of my life. I thank You for Your Love, Grace, Mercy, Faithfulness, Friendship, Presence, and above all Salvation. I thank You for teaching me the importance of giving thanks to You in all things every day. As I dedicate this book to You, I thank You for blessing the readers. I pray that they will be encouraged, enlightened, enriched, and edified in every way by this testimony and teaching. In Jesus' Name I pray. Amen

SINNER'S PRAYER

Father, I confess that Your Son, Jesus is LORD and Savior. I believe in my heart that He died on the Cross for my sins and You raised Him from the dead. I repent of my sins and ask that You would forgive me. Because I am saved, I thank you for my Salvation. Now, Father show me YOU that I may become the son or daughter in the earth that You have called, chosen, and destined me to be. In Jesus' Name I pray. Amen

ACKNOWLEDGEMENTS

This book is dedicated to the honor and Glory of the only true, real and Living God. It is also dedicated to the memory of my beloved parents, Lillie Mae and Willie. I thank my niece Bernice who assisted and supported me in the completion of this book. Many thanks to my spiritual covering, Apostle H. Daniel Wilson, Senior Pastor of Valley Kingdom Ministries International. I also thank Reverend Dr. Donald L. Parson, Senior Pastor of the Logos Baptist Assembly Church. I thank those who work with me in ministry who encourage me to continue in the work of the LORD and all my loyal supporters who have purchased the books I have written over the years and allowed the words I have penned to minister to them.

ABOUT THE AUTHOR

Dr. Herstine Wright resides in Chicago, IL. She loves God and has a heart for serving His people. A proven leader in her community, she co-founded the Operation Put It Back! Coalition (Rebuilders, Repairers, Restorers) in 2005, formed to restore prayer in public schools, ultimately to change a generation. She is also co-founder and executive director of Advocates of Change, a non-for-profit organization. Since the organization's inception, it has awarded many scholarships to children in private and public schools for their high scholastic achievements. Because she is a prolific and energetic trailblazer in her own 'right' and extremely passionate about winning souls for Christ and giving back to the community, she co-founded S.A.L.T.E.D. (Saving A Life To End Destruction), an Evangelistic Outreach Ministry, to offer a solution to the systemic problem of violence that is prevalent in Chicago neighborhoods. The ministry reaches out to men and women involved in gangs and drug activity by offering them a positive alternative to their plight. It also serves homeless men, women, and children. She is the CEO of WriHers Ink and SFP companies. Herstine has written over eight Christian books, and she is also a songwriter. She is a retired community college educator and holds a Ph.D. in Biblical Studies; Master of Arts in English; Master of Science in Vocational Education, and a Bachelor of Arts in Business, with emphasis in teaching Business Education courses. She has been a faithful member of Valley Kingdom Ministries International Church for more than 25 years. Occasionally, she serves as 'guest teacher/speaker' for several ministries.

INTRODUCTION

In my search for God many years ago, not only did I find Him, but I have discovered how amazing it is to live in His manifest Presence. Equally important is to hear His Voice speaking daily. Of this very thing, I have testified in many of the books I have written over the years. No money, fame, nor fortune can compare with having the LORD's touch, embrace, and above all, hearing His Voice on a continual basis. God is a Great God; and as awesome as He is, I have discovered that He desires His Creation, particularly mankind, to love on Him and to appreciate Him. This, of course, stems from hearing His Voice revealing how important it is to Him. It also includes positioning ourselves to <u>KNOW</u> *<u>Him</u>* and not just to KNOW of Him or KNOW about Him. Convinced of that very fact so profoundly, the Holy Spirit compelled me to pen this book, *The Power of KNOW in the Word, Worship, and Works.* As I attempt to tap into the heart and the mind of God daily, I am also reminded of the Scripture which Paul encourages the believer to do in his letter to the church of Ephesus—*"Find out what is pleasing to the LORD"* (Ephesians 5:10). He later reveals his earnest desire, *"that I may know him and the power of his resurrection, and may share his sufferings, becoming like him in his death"* (Philippians 3:10). My heart's desire is to find out what makes God happy with the life that I live for Him— and that is to please Him. Above all, my desire is to *KNOW* Him. *The Power of KNOW* will not only reveal how hearing the Voice of God brings KNOWLEDGE, but how that KNOWLEDGE becomes *Power* and how that *Power* is active in the *Word* of God,

Introduction

in our *Worship,* and in our *Works*. It is that *KNOWLEDGE* that transcends into *Power* which causes us to be victorious in every area of our lives. As people of God, we have been ordained to walk in *KNOWLEDGE* and to <u>*KNOW*</u> that our *KNOWLEDGE* has *Power*. In frequent conversations with people, we often say, "I Know Her, Him, or Them". We may have seen that person only once, but when we recall that individual to mind, we quickly assert, "I Know Her, Him, or Them", when we actually have no information about who the person is. We can identify them and put a name with their face, but we have no real relationship with the person and, therefore, no real understanding of who he/she is. So, we use the word *KNOW* very vaguely. The *KNOW* that I make reference to in this book is predicated not only in the written *Word* of God, but what the LORD has spoken to me personally. So, I rightly say, "I <u>*KNOW*</u> Because He Told Me So". Consequently, for the purpose of clarity, we will define the word *KNOW* as <u>SURETY</u>. When we are <u>*SURE*</u> of a person, thing, or situation, we are convinced, certain, positive; more than anything, we are persuaded. There is no doubt in our minds that it is TRUTH, and no one or anything can convince us otherwise. The LORD desires to speak <u>SURETY</u> to His People so that they become *KNOWERS* of Him!

I pray this book will not only give you, the reader, additional insight, but it will bless you and cause you to climb greater heights and go to deeper depths in your relationship with God as you enjoy a walk and a fellowship with Him like never before. When we become knowledgeable of the *Word* of God, give the LORD 'real' *Worship*, and, of course, do the *Works* to advance the Kingdom of God, we walk in PURPOSE. Our PURPOSE is to glorify God in any and all things

Introduction

and circumstances. In order to glorify Him, it is imperative that we come into a full revelation of who the LORD is. In other words, we must *KNOW* Him. For I am convinced that God has *PURPOSED* His people to be about advancing His Kingdom, and our *KNOW* is a significant part of it.

PART I

For *Purpose*

CHAPTER 1
Mankind's Purpose

The writer of Proverbs (Solomon) clearly states that *"Many are the plans in the mind of a man, but it is the purpose of the LORD that will be established" (19:21)*. According to the above passage, no matter what plans we have for our lives as a people, if it is contrary to God's, it will not prevail. God has revealed to some of us our individual *purpose* very clearly. Yet, there are many people who are desperately looking for the real reason God placed them in His Earth. Even though this appears to be a cumbersome task, God has made it very plain to every human being his/her REAL *purpose*; and it is outlined in His Word. In the book of Acts as Paul meets the Athenians who were worshiping the 'unknown god', he did not leave them hanging. He tells them where they had errored. Immediately, he declared the 'unknown god' to them. Not only did Paul explain who God was, but he clearly outlined God's *purpose* for all mankind. Here is what he says,

> *And he made from one man every nation of mankind to live on all the face of the earth, having determined allotted periods and the boundaries of their dwelling place, that they should seek God, and perhaps feel after him and find him. Yet he is not far from each of us, for in him we live and move and have our being.*
>
> *(Acts 17:24-29)*

If we would examine the above Scripture and take it to heart, I believe, without a doubt, we will ascertain what is the most important reason for every human being's existence. It is clearly to 'Seek God,' 'Feel after Him' and 'Find Him'. Surely, above anything else, it is every human being's *purpose* throughout the entire world, no matter what nationality or ethnicity. No other *purpose* matters if we have not performed that one duty—to 'Seek God', 'Feel God', and 'Find God.' Ironically, Paul prioritizes the order in which it is done. We first seek Him. One may ask, "How Is That Done?" If we are looking for the Great King, we must diligently posture ourselves to pray, study the Word of God, meditate on the Word of God, and praise and worship Him daily. There are no 'ifs', 'ands', or 'buts'. That's the way we do it! We may have to wrestle with the LORD while **<u>diligently</u>** seeking Him. I personally don't believe that we can grab a hold of the LORD <u>fully</u> until we have wrestled with Him. Jacob, the son of Isaac, had a physical encounter with Him. Ours is not; it is spiritual. The tenacity and intensity of the wrestle will determine whether we win the fight. The wrestle has no effect unless we win the fight— Get God! In other words, a 'Wrestle' Has No 'Avail' or Power Unless It *'Prevails'*. Jacob received the blessing because he won the fight—He prevailed! (Genesis 32:24-29). Let me parenthetically say that not only must we *prevail* or come out the winner as we seek God, but we must win over people too. It is important to note that Jacob did not *prevail* over JUST the angel of God in the wrestle but with men also. For one, Jacob *prevailed* over his uncle Laban who had used him for 20 or more years to labor for one of his daughters, Rachel. He did not repay Laban for his subtle, selfish ways. He humbled himself and did as he was told, and God eventually allowed him to outwit him.

Mankind's Purpose

Then he said, "Your name shall no longer be called Jacob, but Israel, for you have striven with God and with men, and have prevailed."

(Genesis 32:28)

As I sought the LORD in my wilderness, I had to wrestle with people too. However, instead of allowing them to remove me from my Godly place, with humility, I exercised 'self-control'. As I stood still, God gave me the victory because He allowed me to *prevail* over them.

In the conversation with the Athenians, Paul continues to explain man's *purpose*—to 'Feel Him'. Certainly, I understand the particular order that Paul presents from my prior experience in seeking, feeling, and finding God. When God sees that we really desire to have Him in our lives, He will reveal Himself—His manifest Presence. The revelation of His manifest Presence, His touch, His embrace, will cause the search to be more intense. We will 'Feel God'. God wants us to 'Feel Him' speaking to us in our physical being—to KNOW how real He is. Lastly, Paul gave the Athenians the final reason for man's existence; and that is to 'Find God' In finding God, we will be ready to surrender our will to Him, humble ourselves to pray and obey Him, and more than anything, come to KNOW Him. The intensity of the search will cause us to want more and more of Him because we have FOUND HIM! So, while we ponder over why God put us on this Earth, we will surely *KNOW* after we SEEK God, FEEL God, and FIND God, what specifically our *PURPOSE* or assignment is in His Great Plan of Salvation. With that revelation, we will *KNOW* the 'real' reason the Great God placed us in the Earth; and to that end, nothing else really matters.

CHAPTER 2
Appearance

It is great to *KNOW* that we have a loving and kind God who wants to interact with His people in such a special way. Being in His manifest Presence, I am convinced that He wants to be 'that kind of Friend' because He has revealed it. For this reason, David encourages in Scripture, *"Seek the LORD and his strength, seek his presence continually!" (I Chronicles 16:11)* For David knew that the Presence of God is the divine place where the LORD's Strength can be found and His Voice heard. He also reveals that it is the path of life. *"Thou dost show me the path of life; in thy presence there is fullness of joy..." (Psalms 16:11)* Many of God's people are searching for this path and even joy, not realizing that it is found in the LORD's manifest Presence. God has *purpose* for our coming into this great communion with Him. If the believers have not yet gotten into His Presence, it will be cumbersome for them to come into an understanding of the LORD's *purpose* for revealing Himself nor will they understand what their *purpose* is. I remember traveling by automobile and the LORD ministering these words, "I Have Called You To Ministry". Even though that was a general statement, I was content with those words. Just the fact that He spoke to me gave me great joy. I was elated that He had called me to serve in His Kingdom! Later, He revealed that I was chosen to be a witness for Him in the Earth. As I continued to seek His Face and became closer, He was more specific with my assignments. The Apostle Paul's *purpose* was revealed by God when He appeared to him on the road to Damascus. When he appeared before King Agrippa, Paul shared his testimony of his initial encounter with Jesus. As he recounts his dialogue with Divinity, he says,

> *And I said, 'Who are you, LORD?' And the LORD said, I am Jesus whom you are persecuting. But rise and stand upon your feet; for I have appeared to you for this purpose, to appoint you to serve and bear witness to the things in which you have seen me and to those in which I will appear to you...*
>
> *(Acts 26:15-16)*

When the LORD appeared to Paul, it, no doubt, changed his entire life. He left with knowledge and his *purpose*. We can conclude that as we continually seek the LORD and His Strength, and His Presence, the LORD will appear to us and reveal more <u>specifically</u> our *purpose* in the Kingdom.

CHAPTER 3
Preservation

As the LORD reveals Himself for a specific purpose, He also *preserves* His people for His *Purpose*. No doubt, we are still alive because God has *preserved* us. As I write this book, many of us in the world today are witnessing something that we have never seen before. We are in the midst of a plague/pestilence, a pandemic (Corona Virus/COVID-19), that is stalking the Earth and killing millions of people daily with no natural panacea in sight. In spite of this deadly virus, I believe that God will *preserve* a remnant for His *Purpose*. Consequently, we are not to *fear the pestilence that stalks in the darkness (Psalms 91:3)* because we must believe that our God has *preserved* us for His *Purpose*. I remember the LORD ministering this word to me a few weeks prior to the announcement of the COVID-19 pandemic that "I Am Safe Under His Wings, Just As Long As I STAY". I also reminded the LORD with these words, "I Don't Plan To Go Anywhere But STAY!" I am also mindful of a passage in the Bible that validates the fact that the LORD *preserves* those He has specifically called for *purpose* regardless of how bad the situation may look.

In the book of Numbers, there was a group of rebels that challenged Moses' and Aaron's authority and likened themselves to them. In other words, they thought that Moses and Aaron were not the 'chosen' ONLY, and they were 'lording' themselves over them. These were the leading, chosen men from the tribes of Levi and Ruben, specifically called Korah and company. While they complained against Moses and Aaron, being clearly out of order, they presented their offerings before the LORD. Here is what Scripture says happened to the rebels,

> *These are the Dathan and Abiram, chosen from the congregation, who contended against Moses and Aaron in the company of Korah, when they contended against the LORD, and the earth opened its mouth and swallowed them up together with Korah, when that company died, when the fire devoured two hundred and fifty men; and they became a warning. Notwithstanding, the sons of Korah did not die.*
>
> *(Numbers 26:9-11)*

After God wiped Korah, the others, and their families off the face of the Earth, as terrible and horrific this warning was to the rest of the Israelites, He *preserved* the sons of Korah. The sons of Korah did not perish with the rest of his household. One would ask, "Why were the sons of Korah spared when God killed the wives, children, animals, and entire households of these other men who participated in this evil?" "After all, the sons of Korah belonged to the family of the leader of the rebellion." Later, after carefully examining Scripture, I discovered that the reason the sons of Korah were spared was because they were *preserved* for God's specific *purpose*. They were chosen to be worship leaders, songwriters, and psalmists in the service of the LORD. As a matter of fact, many of their songs are listed in the Book of Psalms (42-49, 84, 85, 87, 88). The LORD knew what He had placed in them specifically for Him; therefore, He *preserved* them.

Preservation

Even the evil that their father had done before God was not enough to eradicate the *purpose* God had ordained for them in His service because *The LORD God Preserves His People For His Purpose!*

CHAPTER 4
'Fully'

In my walk with the LORD, I have come to the realization and revelation that the LORD has need of *'fully'* people for His *Purpose*. He reveals it in several passages of the Holy Bible. Joshua and Caleb were blessed to enter the land of Promise because the LORD saw their faith and confidence in Him. They were *'fully'*/wholly people. They 'wholly' followed the LORD (Numbers 32:12). Because the LORD seeks *'fully'* people, for these reasons, He puts His *KNOW* in them because He realizes that it is the only sure way He can have ALL of them. The LORD always wanted a people whom He could call 'My People'—ones whom He claims as His and His only. After all, the LORD's portion is His People (Deuteronomy 32:9). For these reasons, He chose the children of Israel out of all the people in the Earth. Even though they angered him occasionally because of their unbelief and constant complaints, He still loved and chose them. He is a jealous God, and according to His Word, He yearns jealously over His Spirit who dwells in us (Exodus 20:5); (Exodus 34:14); (James 4:5). Simply put, He has 'bragging rights', and He wants us **<u>all</u>** to Himself! If we are born-again believers, the LORD cleansed us from our sinful nature so that He could make a people for Himself—those whom He can call 'His'. Our heavenly Father always wanted to make a people for Himself who would worship Him, trust Him, obey Him, fear Him, and above all *KNOW* Him. More than anything, He wanted a people whom He could bless! At times His anger would kindle when the children of Israel would disobey Him and 'break faith' with Him. At one point on the children of Israel's journey out of Egypt, He disowned His People and assigned them to the ownership of Moses. For instance, when Moses left the children of Israel to go up to Mount Sinai to receive the Ten Commandments from God, they were impatient. They encouraged Aaron to build the golden calf that they worshiped, and they were engaged in other riotous behaviors. The LORD heard the bedlam from the camp, and spoke these words to Moses,

> *Go down, because your people, whom you brought up out of Egypt, have become corrupt. They have been quick to turn away from what I commanded them and have made themselves an idol cast in the shape of a calf.*
> *(Exodus 32:7-8)*

The LORD quickly removes Himself from possession of His People, making references to them as *'YOUR People'*—Moses' people—*'whom you brought up out of Egypt'.* The LORD knew *'fully'* well that Moses did not own the Israelites nor could he have brought them up from anywhere without Him. Nonetheless, He separates Himself from them. Because He distances Himself from *His People*, it appears that He is ashamed that He even claims them as His own. However, because we serve a loving, kind, forgiving God who is patient, slow to anger and abounding in mercy, He reclaims them later in the book of Numbers. Because the LORD's anger has subsided, He instructs Moses to tell Aaron and his sons to speak blessings upon them, saying,

'Fully'

May the LORD bless you and cause his face to shine upon you; the LORD lift up his countenance upon you and give you peace. So shall they put my name upon the people of Israel, and I will bless them.
(Numbers 6:24-27)

The LORD wants us to wear His Name and be called *'My People'* so that we are *'fully'* for His use. Needless to say, when we are *'fully'* convinced and persuaded of who the LORD really is, then we can live the life He calls for every believer—*A Life Worthy of HIM*—**Fully** Pleasing to Him! *(Colossians 1:10)*. However, we must be *'fully'* convinced that the LORD is who He says He is. Paul writes to the Romans and says this, *"Each person must be fully convinced in his own mind" (Romans 14:5)*. For the LORD desires His people to be 'sold out' for Him. It comes by way of our studying and meditating on the *Word* of God, coupled with spending time with the King. Concurring with Paul, I too have discovered in my walk with the LORD and living in His manifest Presence daily that He desires *'fully'* convinced people— *in their mind.* That was the primary reason the Savior died for us. It was about the mind. According to Scripture in the Old Testament, the sacrifice of the blood of animals given as an offering for the sins of people dealt with ablutions, the cleansing of the body, things they were forbidden to touch or eat without being defiled, etc. However, there was no sacrifice for the conscience (mind) of people. That was the purpose of Jesus' sacrifice—the shedding of His Blood. Jesus died to 'perfect' our conscience. He purified our conscience that we could keep a 'clear conscience' in serving God (Romans 9:1);

(I Peter 3:16); (1 Timothy 3:9). In other words, He wants us to be *'fully'* convinced in our minds that He is who He says He is. Unfortunately, there are so-called believers who profess to be believers; but they are not *'fully'* convinced that our God is who He says He is. Sadly, they don't KNOW it. I have heard some, as they defended the rights of other people's beliefs say, "Everybody has a right to believe what he/she wants". "Who is to say that what they believe is not right". Certainly, everyone does have a right to believe whatever he/she desires. God gives us that individual freedom. However, when so-called saved individuals believe that other people may be right, that is a direct contradiction to what we believe. It is clear that they are NOT *'fully'* convinced of the Truth nor their faith in God. They also open a portal for the devil to bring his ideologies, philosophies, and lies to corrupt their minds. If we are not *'fully'* convinced, we will become like Micah, one who is mentioned in the book of Judges. Micah possessed in his house a priest, whom he ordained, an ephod, a teraphim, and a graven image all at the same time. What a contradiction! Micah also became indignant when members of the tribe of Dan stole them from his house. When he confronts them, He says this, *"You take my gods, which I made, and the priest, and go away, and what have I left?" (Judges 18:24).* Unfortunately, these were God's people who were *'Fence Straddlers'*; but they did not know it. They were a generation whose parents/ancestors did not leave them a 'spiritual inheritance'. They were not as the tribe of Gadites, Reubenites, and the Manassites who built and altar to the LORD as they focused on the 'spiritual inheritance' for their children and the generations after them (Joshua 22:10-34). They wanted

'Fully'

their children to *KNOW* that the LORD God is God, so they built and altar and called it 'Witness'. *"For said they, 'it is a witness between us that the LORD is God'" (Joshua 22:10-34).* As believers and saints of the Most High God, we have an obligation to *KNOW* God ourselves and teach our children so that they do not become unbelievers nor *'Fence Straddling'* believers. In the book of I Kings, the prophet Elijah poses this question to God's people while they were *'Fence Straddling'*, "How long will you go limping with two opinions" If the LORD is God follow him but if Baal, then follow him" (18:21). God does not want *'Fence Straddling'* believers! He clearly expresses that fact in the book of Revelation, *"So, because you are lukewarm, and neither hot nor cold, I will spit you out of my mouth" (Revelation 3:16).* We cannot believe the Holy Bible and The Quran concurrently. It is one or the other. When we are *'fully'* convinced that we have the 'real Truth', then we become the 'oak of Righteousness', 'the planting of the LORD', whom God describes in the book of Isaiah. And it is the 'planting of the LORD' that brings Glory to His Wonderful Name (Isaiah 61:1-3). The LORD also looks for the *'fully'* heart. He says these words in the book of 2 Chronicles, *"For the eyes of the LORD run to and fro throughout the earth to show Himself strong on behalf of those whose heart is fully devoted to Him" (16:9).* Without question, the LORD seeks a *'fully'* devoted heart. For the LORD knows that when our hearts are *'fully'* devoted to Him, we are loyal and, therefore, can be trusted. A trustworthy servant is His Heart's desire.

We are also encouraged to set our minds, *"Set your minds on things that are above not on things that are on earth" (Colossians 3:2).* Being *'fully'* convinced that the LORD is who

He says He is requires a 'set mind'. A 'set mind' can be slightly compared to the manner in which we set a radio in our vehicle to listen to our favorite stations, a DVD to record our favorite movies, watches and clocks when time changes, or a plethora of other things we do on a daily basis. We have gadgets we use or buttons that we press that enable us to perform such tasks. However, a few of those tasks may change at any given moment, day, week, month, or even year. Unlike the gadgets we use, a 'set mind' for God, *'fully'* convinced that He is who He says He is, cannot be altered at any time. Once it is set, it is immovable. God blesses us when we give Him a 'set mind'. This is what the angel reveals to Daniel from an answered prayer,

> *Then he said to me, 'Fear not, Daniel, for from the first day that you set your mind to understand and humbled yourself before your God, your words have been heard, and I have come because of your words.'*
>
> (Daniel 10:12)

The focus here is the fact that Daniel 'set' his mind. He didn't waiver; he wanted to understand what God's plan was for him and the people who were in exile and the time of their release. Moreover, he humbled himself. He refused to let anyone or anything take or shift his focus. He was determined to hear the Voice of God and *KNOW* what He was speaking to him. He was *'fully'* convinced that God would also deliver on His promise. We can conclude that to *KNOW* the LORD and walk in our individual assignments, we, too, must avail ourselves *'fully'* for the LORD's *Purpose* and believe that He will deliver on His promises.

CHAPTER 5
'Called'

*B*eing *'fully'* convinced that God is indeed The LORD, and He is above all, through all, and in all, we should be inclined to believe that there is a mighty *'Call'* on the believers' lives to fulfill. Therefore, we should be *'fully'* convinced that God will fulfill *His Purpose* for each one of His children. It is not for the work entirely but to receive the promises that He has made available that are ready to be released. A passage from the book of Acts reminds us,

> *For the promise is unto you, and to your children, and to all that are afar off, even as many as the LORD our God shall call.*
>
> *(Acts 2:39)*

No doubt, the LORD's *'Call'* is for *purpose*. It is for those who believe that He is the Son of God and He died for their sins and the Father raised Him from the dead. However, how we receive the promises, will be contingent upon us. God has always 'placed the ball in our court'. We, the believers, determine how the promises will be manifest or how the promises will come to fruition. In other words, 'sure promises' are contingent on our obedience to God—our actions. This is what the LORD says about the promises concerning Abraham,

Abraham will surely become a great and powerful nation, and all nations on earth will be blessed through him. For I have chosen him, so that he will direct his children and his household after him to keep the way of the LORD by doing what is right and just, so that the LORD will bring about for Abraham what he has promised him.
(Genesis 18:18-19)

We are the chosen, the *'Called'*; and God is willing, ready to direct us to our specific *purpose* and to fulfill the promises He made to Abraham and to us. We can rightly conclude that God's people become role players in the manifestations of the promises of God.

A Purposeful Walk in KNOWING His Ways

One of the things the LORD mentions in His promise to Abraham is that Abraham would direct his children and his household after him to *keep the way of the LORD,* and that is clearly by *doing what is right and just.* There is another passage of Scripture that reminds us of this very fact, *"That God—his way is perfect..." (Psalms 18:30).* His *Way* is perfect because the LORD is The *Way!* Well, before anyone can *Keep the LORD's Way*, it is equally important that an individual *KNOWS His Way/Ways.* For it can be detrimental to a people and generation not to be knowledgeable of the LORD's Ways. He expresses His displeasure as He speaks to Moses,

Therefore, I was provoked with that generation, and said, 'They always go astray in their heart; they have not known my ways.'
(Hebrews 3:10)

'Called'

In Deuteronomy 32:4, the LORD defines His *Ways* by saying, *"The Rock, his work is perfect, for all his ways are justice. A God of faithfulness and without iniquity, just and upright is he".* According to the above passage, to *KNOW* the LORD's Way/*Ways* is simply to *KNOW* Him! Anyone who does not have the revelation of the LORD, His Way/*Ways*, does not have a revelation of who He is. As finite creatures of God, we want people whom we come in contact with on a regular basis—our friends, family, co-workers, etc., to *KNOW* who we are. We desire that they *KNOW* our character, personality, our likes and dislikes. In other words, we want them to *KNOW* what makes us laugh, what makes us frown, what good deeds we do for others so that they will know the type of individuals they are dealing with, being careful not to reveal our weaknesses. We believe that if people *KNOW* who we are, they would *KNOW* how to treat us with kindness and respect. We are often disappointed when they have a tendency to play on our weaknesses and emotions. Similarly, the LORD wants us to *KNOW* Him. Unlike us, the LORD has no weaknesses. But He has feelings! He wants us to *KNOW* that He is a Good God and that we serve an amazing, kind-hearted, merciful, caring God. That is why He spoke these words through the prophet Jeremiah,

> *Thus says the LORD, Let not the wise man boast in his wisdom, let not the mighty man boast in his might, let not the rich man boast in his riches, but let who boasts boast in this, that he understands and knows me, that I am the LORD who practices steadfast love, justice, and righteousness in the earth. For in these things I delight, declares the LORD.*
>
> *(Jeremiah 9:23-24)*

THE POWER OF KNOW

The above Scripture clearly reveals *His Ways*/His Practice—that the LORD is merciful, gracious, faithful; and more than anything, He wants His children to boast about it and to *KNOW* it! As we come into the full knowledge of the LORD's Ways, then we will have a better understanding of who we are. In other words, as He reveals His identity, we will *KNOW* our identity. As the LORD reveals our identity, we will *KNOW* we have been *'called'* for *purpose*. The Apostle Paul encourages us as he wrote to the church in Ephesus these words,

> *I therefore, a prisoner for the LORD, beg you to lead a life worthy of the calling to which you have been called, with all lowliness and meekness, with patience, forebearing one another in love, eager to maintain the unity of the Spirit in the bond of peace.*
>
> *(Ephesians 4:1-3)*

KNOWING that we have a *'call'* to fulfill and to be sure of our *'call'* (2 Peter 1:10), we are better able to walk in the *Purpose* the LORD has for us.

PART II

In The *Word*

CHAPTER 6

Empowered or Overpowered?

Without saying, there is a mighty *'call'* on the people of God to *KNOW* the LORD and be acquainted with *His* Ways. On many occasions, we have heard the expression, "Knowledge Is *Power*". I am convinced that it is only *Power* when we search for it, possess it, and properly apply it. Without question, *Knowledge* is found in the *Word* of God. As I constantly study the *Word* of God, I have discovered that people who do not acknowledge God nor believe in Him have gained much *Knowledge* from the Bible. They have accomplished much success in the business world today by applying the principles found in the *Word* of God to gain the prosperity they have. Many of them are unbelievers who have studied the *Word*, gleaned from it, and have become extremely wealthy and successful. Yet, they would not give credit nor attribute their success to God. I am convinced that the LORD has 'willed' a plethora of blessings for His people that we have not collected on because we have not searched the Scriptures nor gotten into His Presence to ascertain what they are. Consequently, they lie dormant in His Kingdom uncollected. God has called His people to have success wherever they go. It is evident in the book of Joshua. After Moses died, God commissioned Joshua to lead the people from the wilderness to the Promise Land. This is what He tells Joshua concerning the *Word*,

THE POWER OF KNOW

This book of the law shall not depart out of your mouth, but you shall meditate on it day and night, that you may be careful to do according to all that is written in in it; for then you shall make your way prosperous, and then you shall have good success.

(Joshua 1:8)

Indeed, the LORD has given us the recipe for success, and it is in the *Word* of God. When we acquire the *Knowledge* in the *Word* of God, meditate on it, obey it, and apply it, then our KNOW has Power. His Word declares that, *"My people perish for lack of knowledge" (Hosea 4:6).* This Scripture is indicative of the fact that death is associated with being deficient in the *Knowledge* of God. He continues by saying, *"because you have rejected knowledge, I reject you from being a priest to me" (Hosea 4:6).* If we are a born-again believer, we are automatically priests of the Most High God. *"We are a chosen people, royal priesthood, a holy nation, God's own possession..." (1 Peter 2:9).* It is apparent in the preceding passage that there were people of God who were dressed in the priestly garments delivering the Word of God Sunday after Sunday, Wednesday after Wednesday. However, they rejected the *Knowledge* of God and were still serving in their priestly capacity. According to the *Word* that the prophet Hosea delivered to the people, their contributions were NOT received by God. Thank God that Jesus presents us as Godly priests before the Father when we have been 'slow' in attaining the *Knowledge* of God. Even though Jesus stands in our place, we still have a duty and responsibility to *KNOW* the LORD. For these reasons the LORD tells us to *"Be still and know that I am God"*

Empowered or Overpowered?

(Psalms 46:10). The LORD also requires the believer to increase daily in the *Knowledge* of His Word. When the Apostle Paul prays for the church in Colossae, in his prayer, He mentions the three requirements that describe *living a life worthy of the LORD*—one is to, '*increase daily in the Knowledge of Him*' *(Colossians 1:10)*. According to Paul's prayer, if we are not *increasing daily in the knowledge of the LORD,* we are not living a life worthy of Him. When we allow the Spirit of Truth to add to our *Knowledge* daily, it is then and only then that the *Word* becomes our guiding light/direction, '*a lamp to our feet and a light to our path*' *(Psalms 119:105)*; and we are *Empowered*. Of course, we are *Empowered* by the *Word* when we obey the *Word* of God. In other words, we must be 'doers' of the *Word* as God's servant James encourages us to do (James 1:22). When we obey the *Word* of God, we walk in the *Knowledge* of the Truth, which is the *Word* of God. I believe, however, we have not allowed the *Word* to do what God intended it to do and be—*Power!*—because we have not studied it. Many believers use several pretexts for not studying it. As a matter of fact, I have even heard a believer say in a prayer, "I don't know Scripture but I KNOW you." I find it cumbersome to conceive the fact that one can *KNOW* God and not *KNOW* His *Word* when He is the *Word*!

Not only is the *Word* our guiding light and a lamp to our feet and *Power*, but it is LIFE. If we do not *KNOW* the *Word*, we have no LIFE. We have heard the expression, "You Need To Get A Life!", from those who would disparage one's life or behavior if his/her performance does not live up to the standards of what they deem 'living'. God clearly defines LIFE as His Word. When He spoke to Moses concerning His

THE POWER OF KNOW

Laws and His People, He said this,

> *See I set before you this day life and good, death and evil. If you obey the commandments of the LORD your God which I command you this day, by loving the LORD your God, by walking in his ways, and by keeping his commandments, and his statues and his ordinances, then you shall live and multiply, and the LORD your God will bless you in the land which you are entering to take possession of it.*
> *(Deuteronomy 30:15-16)*

In essence, the LORD was saying that if we obey His words, we will have LIFE; if we do not obey, we will have death. When we are *Empowered* by the *Word*, we choose LIFE and we walk in *Power*. When we do not, we choose death and become *Overpowered* by the devil. We may not die physically, but we become dead spiritually. We may have the very appearance of LIFE, but we are dead. Moreover, we would have allowed the devil to give us a false sense of the definition of LIFE. When I purchased my first home, I remember planting a beautiful shrubbery in my yard. Over the years, I watched it grow until it became a beautiful tree with purple leaves. Five years later, I noticed how a weed, which looked like a tree, had taken root in between my tree's bark. As much as I worked to get that weed from between my tree, it continued to grow. Later, I discovered that my beautiful purple-leaf tree had become a dry leafless tree with only a stump. The weed had killed the tree and stood in its place, and it had begun to look like a tree. Even today when the landscaper trims it, he is convinced that it is a real tree when I KNOW it is a weed. Just like my purple-leaf tree had been *Overpowered*, I believe, without a doubt, that many people have been *Overpowered* by the devil because they refuse to be *Empowered* by the *Word* of God. They are standing as a beautiful tree, but they are actually a weed with the appearance of a beautiful tree. They are filled with a false alacrity. They have great friends, employment, businesses, homes, mates, etc, but they are unhappy, LIFELESS people! We, the believers, must be careful that we don't become weeds, looking as if we are beautiful trees. When we do not allow the *Word* to get inside of us to *Empower* us—grow us, mature us, and CHANGE us, we will become *Overpowered* by the enemy and live a frivolous life with the appearance of LIFE. God wants us to *KNOW* the *Word* that we may be *Empowered* by the *Word* and live the 'abundant life'.

CHAPTER 7
If Demons *KNOW,* Why Don't The Believers?

As we become *Empowered* by the *Word* of God, no doubt, we will *KNOW* the *Power* that it has, being careful not to become like those who Apostle Paul described in the book of 2 Timothy, *"as having the appearance of godliness, but denying its power" (3:5).* He even warns us to eschew them! No doubt, the *Word* is powerful. It is powerful because it is the LORD. The writer of Hebrew describes the *Power* of the *Word* of God in this manner,

> *The word of God is quick, and powerful, and sharper than any two edged sword, piercing even to the dividing asunder of soul and spirit, and of the joints and marrow, and is a discerner of the thoughts and intents of the heart!*
> *(Hebrews 4:12)*

In the gospel of John, these words are written, *"And the word became flesh to dwell among us" (John 1:14).* Jesus is the *Word*, and He is *Power*! *KNOWING* Him means we walk in that *Power*. Being knowledgeable of this Truth, it seems elusive to give credence to the fact that an evil spirit would be more knowledgeable of the LORD than a child of God and even recognize Him on site. Unfortunately, it is the truth. When Jesus walked in the Earth doing miracles, signs, and wonders, I often wondered why every encounter He had with demonic forces, they KNEW who He was.

> *And when he saw Jesus from a far, he ran and fell down before him. And crying out with a loud voice, he said, "What have you to do with me, Jesus, Son of the Most High God? I adjure you by God, do not torment me."*
> *(Mark 5:6-7)*

In accordance with the previous Scripture, it is very discouraging and much to the believers' chagrin to allow a demon to recognize and have the revelation of who Jesus is, and they do not. Even more disheartening is to allow a demon to be so acquainted with Jesus that it would engage Jesus in conversation and even ask Him for a special favor. God's favor is for His beloved. However, that is what happened. As people of God, we must realize that God put us on the Earth, as referenced in a previous chapter, to SEEK, FEEL, and FIND Him that we may *KNOW* Him. I do not believe that it was the LORD's intention nor His Will to be in a discussion with demons. On many occasions, Jesus would forbid them even to speak.

> *And demons also came out of many, crying, "You are the Son of God!" But he rebuked them and would not allow them to speak, because they knew that he was the Christ.*
> *(Luke 4:41)*

Sadly, the demons KNEW Jesus was the Christ, and many believers do not *KNOW* it. Jesus sets the record straight that dialoguing with the LORD is reserved for His children, not demons! Unfortunately, many of His children have relinquished that privilege. They fail to utilize it because they are loath to get into the LORD's Glorious Presence. If we are students of the *Word* of God, we should be familiar with the Sons of Sceva and their encounter and horrific experience with the demons as they attempted to cast them out. *"But the evil spirit answered them, "Jesus I know, and Paul I recognize, but who are you?" (Acts 19:15).* Vessels that do not *KNOW* the Truth open themselves up to demonic attacks. They are easy targets because demons know they are no apparent threat to them. Their assignment is very clear, to discard the Truth. They prey on the vulnerable because they are easily assessable, and they use them at their pleasure. In the book of Timothy, the Apostle Paul expresses his displeasure with how the weak and vulnerable were taken advantage of, via false teachings. He specifically points to a certain clientele. He says,

> *For among them are those who creep into households and capture weak women, burdened with sins and led astray by various passions, always learning and never able to arrive at a knowledge of the truth.*
> *(2 Timothy 3:6-7)*

To preclude God's people from becoming a victim of prey, Paul warns them of the danger and ramification they will encounter when they are deficient in the Truth. According to Paul, these people's learning became a vicious cycle. Because of the cycle, they never came into the full knowledge of the Truth. As we walk with Jesus daily, and as we take His Yoke upon us and learn of Him (Matthew 11:29), we are protected from demonic influence. For we have the Precious Blood of Jesus and the Word of Truth, the gospel of our Salvation. However, it will be incumbent upon us to guard the Truth we receive (2 Timothy 1:14). Surely, demons recognize those who carry the spirit of Christ as they did Jesus Himself. When the devil accosted Jesus in the wilderness and dialogued with Him very intensely, the devil was very familiar with the *Word* of God, and he quoted Scripture (Matthew 4:6-10). Demons are constantly at work to gain an advantage over God's people and to preclude them from performing and carrying out God's mission in the Earth. For the devil's intent is very clear. He wants the believers' KNOW because there is *Power* that is attached to it!

Surely, the LORD has allowed the devil to know SOME things. However, God has given *KNOW Power* only to His children—the *Power* in His *Word* and His Presence that says we are victorious and we have the *Power* to tread over the devil and his imps!

CHAPTER 8
The *Author* and *Teacher* Inside

In several passages of Scriptures in the *Word* of God, the LORD encourages and articulates very clearly that *Belief* is what gives us access to the Kingdom. For instance, to become saved, we must believe in our hearts and confess with our mouths that Jesus Christ is the Son of God and that He died on the Cross and God raised Him from the dead. With that confession, God promises that we are saved from hell, forgiven of our sins, and have eternal life. For these reasons, it is imperative that we **Believe**, which is also powerful. For the LORD reminds us that all things are possible if we believe (Mark 9:23). However, it is the LORD's intent to make <u>*KNOWERS*</u> out of His people. For the LORD desires to transition us from Belief to *KNOW* to increase our faith. Jesus admonished one of His disciples who made a request that He would show them the Father, and he and the other disciples would be pleased. However, Jesus responds with these words, *"Have I been with you so long, and yet you do not know me, Phillip?" (John 14:9).* It is here that Jesus admonishes Phillip for his failure to KNOW Him after He had spent an elongated time with Him. By this time, according to Jesus, he should have known that He and the Father were One.

Throughout the *Word* of God, the LORD constantly mentions the word *KNOW*. Not only does the LORD mention *KNOW*, but He appears to be pleading with His people not to *KNOW* about Him, but to *KNOW* HIM! In the book of Ezekiel,

THE POWER OF KNOW

there are a myriad of passages that speak to that very fact. The LORD's constant words to His people as He would discipline them were, "That they will *KNOW* that I am the LORD, God" (Ezekiel 20:20; 20:26; 20:37; 20:42; 20:44; 22:16; 23:24; 24:27; 25:5; 25:7; 25:11; 25:17; 26:6; 28-36). The LORD reiterates these words in other passages in the Word of God as well. For instance, in the book of Jeremiah, He expresses His displeasure with His people by saying, *"They refuse to know me" (Jeremiah 9:6)*. In another passage, the prophet Isaiah speaks these words, *"The ox knows its owner, and the donkey its master's crib, but Israel does not know, my people do not understand" (Isaiah 1:3)*. The LORD contrasts the disdain and the disrespect His people exemplified toward Him with the loyalty and respect an animal shows to its master. In essence, the animals <u>knew</u> who their masters were and obeyed them; but His people who were called by His Name did not have a clue of who He was; and they disobeyed Him. The animals *knew* to whom they belonged and where their provisions emanated from, but His people failed to realize. Because His people were disloyal by refusing to *KNOW* Him, He appears to do something different. He had the prophet Jeremiah to pen these words,

> *For this is the covenant that I will make with the house of Israel after those days, declares the LORD: I will put my law within them, and I will write it on their hearts. And I will be their God, and they shall be my people. And no longer shall each one teach his neighbor and each his brother, saying, 'Know the LORD', for they shall all know me, from the least of them to the greatest, declares the LORD. For I will forgive their iniquity, and I will remember their sin no more.*
>
> *(Jeremiah 31:33-34)*

The *Author* and *Teacher* Inside

In the previous passage, the LORD is very explicit. I liken the method that He uses to speak *KNOW* in His People to the manner in which celebrities' names are etched in concrete on the Hollywood Walk of Fame on Hollywood Boulevard located in Hollywood, California. Once written, the names are there forever. Yes, the LORD wants His people to *KNOW* Him to the degree that He is willing to take the pen—His Finger—and become the 'Author' Himself. For He realizes that in order to make His people knowledgeable of HIM, He had to write who He is Himself very plainly on the *INSIDE*. That way, no one will ever doubt His existence and the mere fact that He is who He says He is. In order for that to occur, the LORD has to put His Truth in our inward parts. Perhaps, that is the reason David writes in Psalms, *"Thou desires truth in the inward parts" (51:6).* For the LORD works from the *INSIDE*. God places His Truth in us when we study His *Word* and live in His Presence. Jesus spoke these words to His disciples and others who listened to His teaching, *"If you continue in my word, you are truly my disciples, and you will know the truth, and the truth will set you free" (John 8:31-32).* Truth is powerful, and it is the method which the LORD uses to free us from the bondage of sin. After God led the Israelites out of Egypt, Moses went up to Mount Sinai to receive the Ten Commandments for the children of Israel, Scripture says,

And he gave to Moses, when he had made an end of speaking with him upon Mount Sinai, the two tables of the testimony, tables of stone, written with the finger of God.
(Exodus 31:18)

Like the tables of stones the LORD wrote upon and gave to Moses, the LORD uses His Finger to write upon our hearts. That way, no one with an evil agenda can come behind Him with an 'eraser' and eradicate Him from our hearts. No doubt, the believers' hearts are the new tablets. He assures the believers that the degree in which He will pen His Words on the tablets of their hearts would be so profound that they would no longer need anyone—teacher, preacher, prophet, etc., to teach them to *KNOW* Him; He becomes the *TEACHER* and *WRITER*. No matter how great or small, all will *KNOW* Him! We can conclude that our *KNOW* comes from the ONE who writes and teaches on the *INSIDE* of us! The following Scriptures 'bear witness' to the *'Author/Teacher'* Himself.

> *But the word is very near you; it is in your mouth and in your heart; so that you can do it*
> *(Deuteronomy 30:14).*

> *But the anointing that you received from him abides in you, and you have no need that anyone should teach you. But as his anointing teaches you about everything, and is true, and is no lie— just as it has taught you, abide in him.*
> *(I John 2:27)*

> *I will give you a new heart and put a new spirit in you; I will remove from you your heart of stone and give you a heart of flesh. And I will put my Spirit in you and move you to follow my decrees and be careful to keep my laws.*
> *(Ezekiel 36:26-27)*

The *Author* and *Teacher* Inside

But the Comforter, which is the Holy Ghost, whom the Father will send in my name, he shall teach you all things, and bring all things to your remembrance, whatsoever I have said unto you.

(John 14:26)

<u>Humility for KNOW</u>

It is a blessing to come into an understanding and revelation of the fact that the LORD desires His people to *KNOW* Him so profoundly that He is constantly adding to their *KNOW* daily. That addition comes with being in His manifest Presence. In addition to penning/engraving His laws upon our hearts to bring us into *Knowledge*, He uses *humility*. This particular method may seem cumbersome to process by many people both saved and unsaved, especially when they exemplify 'control' or even pride. For one, *humility* is associated with belittlement, lowliness, meekness. Plainly stated, it means to be humiliated. I cannot think of anyone on planet Earth who desires to be reduced or disparaged or felt 'less than' or simply humiliated. By nature, people desire to be respected and in control; and they are determined that they will not be pushed around nor relegated by another. Yet, the LORD requires His people to conduct themselves with a spirit of *humility*. And He is moved by *humility*. As a matter of fact, He is so moved that he sent a word by His prophet to Ahab, then king of Israel, of the death and destruction that would come upon him and his house for the evil he had done in Israel in causing the people to sin. However, when Ahab humbled himself, this is what God tells the prophet,

"Have you seen how Ahab has humbled himself before me? Because he has humbled himself before me, I will not bring the evil in his days; but in his son's day, I will bring the evil upon his house" (I Kings 21:28-29). Hence, we see that God is a 'softy' to humility! The Word of God reminds us in the book of Proverbs that *humility* precedes honor (15:33). Consequently, if we are seeking honor, we must exemplify *humility* first. I confess in my walk with Christ that it was my *humility* that enabled me to get into the LORD's Presence and remain there. As a matter of fact, applying it to my own life was a great part of my search. Being knowledgeable of that very fact, I keep myself in that posture continually. *Humility* involves exercising self-control or a sound mind. More than anything, it requires possessing wisdom. Here is what James says, *"Who is wise and understanding among you? Let them show it by their good life, by deeds done in the humility that comes from wisdom" (James 3:13).* According to this passage, any deeds that we do for the Kingdom of God has to be done with *humility* and must stem from wisdom. Otherwise, it does not reflect or define a 'good life', nor does it demonstrate that we are wise and understanding. *"When pride comes, then comes disgrace, but with the humble is wisdom" (Proverbs 11:2).* From the preceding passage, it is without question that *humility* and wisdom operate together as one. Therefore, one should not be absent without the other. Possessing *humility* is also a method that the LORD uses to transition His people to the place of *KNOW*. This is what Moses spoke to the Israelites as he reminded them of what God did for them on their journey to the Promise Land,

The *Author* and *Teacher* Inside

And he humbled you and let you hunger and fed you with manna, which you did not know, nor did your fathers know, that he might make you know that man does not live by bread alone, but man lives by every word that comes from the mouth of the LORD.

(Deuteronomy 8:3)

The above passage reveals very concisely that God uses *humility* to teach His people *KNOW*. The Israelites had to experience hunger and be fed with manna for 40 years, unaware that they were dining on the food the angels in heaven feasted on (Psalms 78:24-25). God withheld the favorite delicacies they had enjoyed in Egypt for the many years they were in bondage to give them a different appetite so that they would desire Him. That was, of course, for the purpose of their *KNOWING* that the LORD was their 'Food'. He wanted them to *KNOW* that just having their favorite meals was not sufficient for the life of His people, but He alone. Moses takes his message a bit further by saying, *"that he might make you know"*. Those words paint a vivid portrait of the love that God has for His people. It is clear that God loves His people so dearly and desires for us to *KNOW* the Truth that He takes it upon Himself to *Make Us KNOW*! As the LORD uses *humility to Make Us KNOW*, we are guaranteed a promotion. For He says to, *"Humble yourselves under the mighty hand of God that in due season he may exalt you"* (1 Peter 5:6).

CHAPTER 9
'Tell' and 'Show'

We have discussed how important the *KNOW* of God is for the believer and the *Power* of it in His *Word*. The fact that the LORD is willing to teach us humility, and etch His Laws, His *Word*, in our hearts so intensely that we will never desire to return to our sinful nature or doubt His existence, is extraordinary. As mentioned in the previous chapter, the principal reason that the LORD performs such a miraculous thing for the believer is to transition us from 'Belief to *KNOW*', which strengthens our faith. According to Scripture, we need Faith in order to please God (Hebrews 11:6); and the *KNOW* of God is for the purpose of strengthening/increasing our Faith in Him. One might ask, "What method does the LORD use to write His Words upon our hearts?" For one, He uses the method of *'Tell'* and *'Show'*. What is common to most people is the expression, 'Show and Tell', in that particular order. We are all familiar with the names of games for children and television shows that depict this order. However, the LORD reverses the order as He reveals Himself for the purpose of our *KNOWING* Him. In my walk with the LORD, I have discovered that *KNOW* is not based on what God <u>shows</u> us absolutely; it is what God <u>tells</u> us. Because His reputation is at stake, we should have the faith and confidence in Him that He will deliver, <u>show</u> or perform what He says. For these reasons, it is imperative that the believer not only seeks the Presence of God but **live** in His manifest Presence. In His Presence, He trains us to hear His

Voice and to understand what He says. As we grow and mature in His Presence, we will see the order in which He reveals Himself. When I got into the manifest Presence of the LORD, there were many occasions that He would <u>tell</u> me a thing but would not <u>show</u> me what He had spoken until years later. In the body of Christ, we are so consumed with the *"show me"* theory that we miss what God wants to reveal about Himself. In the book of Exodus, Moses literally pleads with God to *"show me"*, *"show me,"* *"that I may know"*, while God was attempting to reveal His identity <u>FIRST</u>—*"that he might know"*. This is Moses' requests, *"Now therefore, if I have found favor in your sight, please show me now your ways, that I may know you" (Exodus 33:13)*. No doubt, prior to this conversation between the two, Moses had been shown many miraculous things already; but he still did not *KNOW* God. There are many in the body of Christ who probably can testify about how the LORD has blessed them, healed them, provided for them, and a host of other wonderful things He has done. And those are great testimonies. Consequently, they 'know' about God because they have seen Him work, even as Moses did. He simply knew about God. As a matter of fact, the LORD had introduced Himself in His initial encounter with Him with a greeting, "I AM GOD". Further down in the passage, Moses continues to plead with God again to *"show me"*, *"show me"*. Moses said, *"Please show me your glory" (Exodus 33:18)*. In spite of Moses' importunity, God did not relent; He wanted to use His particular order of 'tell' and 'show'. He wanted to 'tell' Moses who He was. He does it by saying these words,

'Tell' and 'Show'

I will make all my goodness pass before you and will proclaim before you my name 'The LORD.' And I will be gracious to whom I will be gracious, and will show mercy on whom I will show mercy.
(Exodus 33:19)

In the previous passage, God <u>tells</u> or gives a definitive presentation to Moses of His Glory by revealing who He is before He <u>shows</u> him His Glory by hiding him in the cleft of the rock as He passes by him and proclaims exactly who He is (Exodus 34:5-7). After that powerful presentation, Moses was convinced without a doubt that he had finally become knowledgeable of this awesome God! It was through the *telling* that he was convinced, not in the *showing*. Moses was *fully convinced* and made a worshiper. It is worth reiterating that he was not made a worshiper because of the awesome miracles God has wrought before his eyes in the plagues of Egypt and the drowning of Pharaoh and his army in the Red Sea, but through the revelation of what the LORD <u>told</u> him as He passed him and proclaimed who He was. Moses believed, *KNEW,* and was prepared to move forth as he continued to lead the children of Israel to the land of Promise (Exodus 34:9). Consequently, we can rightly conclude that our *KNOW* is not predicated solely on what God *shows* us FIRST. Rather, it is based upon what the LORD <u>tells</u> us FIRST that we should believe. Subsequently, it becomes our *KNOW*. With that assurance, we can eradicate the incredulous expression we ofter hear, "I Will Believe It When I See It!" or "I Am From Missouri; You Got To Show Me!" We will have the confidence and above all *KNOW* that the LORD is the kind of God with the reputation that He will deliver on the *Word* He speaks or *tells*.

CHAPTER 10
The *'Tell'* of Two Voices

In a continual discussion of the *Power of KNOW* as it pertains to the *Word*, we should also be mindful that there are several ways the LORD speaks to His people that they might believe Him and, of course, *KNOW* Him. For one, He speaks by way of His *Logos*, the written *Word* and His *Rhema*, which is also the *Word* of God, but not necessarily written. For the sake of clarity, I am referring to both as *The 'Tell' of Two Voices*. I believe the *Logos Word* is the manner in which the LORD initially reveals His Voice to His people. However, there are some to whom He releases His audible. As a young person, I recall my first time actually reading the *Word* of God. The Holy Spirit led me to the gospel of John for a specific reason, and I was enlightened greatly. From that point, I became acquainted with Jesus and desired to learn more. Later, as I matured in Grace, I believed the *Word* and became a student of the *Word*. It has become a 'lamp to my feet and a light to my path'. Without saying, in order to hear the LORD's Voice via the *Logos*/written *Word*, we must study and meditate on the *Word* daily (2 Timothy 2:15) to the point that it is engrained in our very being. Our spirit becomes a data base that we pour into, and we are able to recall and retrieve from it at any moment what the LORD speaks about a certain situation or circumstance. No doubt, His *Word* is He; and it is powerful! (Hebrews 4:12). Aforementioned in a previous chapter, I am convinced that many believers lack *Knowledge* of the things that rightfully belong to them because they have not studied the *Word* of God. God has 'willed' a myriad of blessings for His people that they have neglected because they have not searched the Scriptures nor gotten into His Presence to ascertain what they are. Consequently, the blessings lie dormant in His Kingdom. As I was studying the book of Numbers, there was a passage of Scripture that resonated in my spirit. After the LORD had commanded Moses to allocate the inheritance to the various tribes, there were five ladies who felt that there was an unfair distribution of the inheritance, mainly because their father had no son, thus disqualifying them according to the standards that were set forth. They were being overlooked and, therefore, would not receive their inheritance. What quickened me about this passage was the fact that the ladies took a stand for what they believed. These ladies were the five daughters of Zelophehad of the family of Manasseh, the son of Joseph. This is what Scripture says as they brought their case to Moses and stood before the leaders of Israel and the congregation as well as Eleazar the priest,

> *Our father died in the wilderness; he was not among the company of those who gathered themselves together against the LORD in the company of Korah, but died for his own sin; and he had no sons. Why should the name of our father be taken away from his family because he had no son? Give to us a possession among our father's brethren.*
>
> *(Numbers 27:3-4)*

The *'Tell'* of Two Voices

Apparently, their proposition was a hard decision for Moses to make on his own; so he brought it before the LORD. The LORD deliberated His verdict in favor of the daughters in the matter by saying,

> *The daughters of Zelophehad are right; you shall give them their father's brethren and cause the inheritance of their father to pass to them.*
> *(Numbers 27:7)*

Because these five daughters took a stand for what they believed was 'right', the LORD 'backed' them by agreeing with them. In other words, He told them, *"You Are Right"*. We are encouraged by God Himself to remind Him of what He says in His *Word* through the prophet Isaiah. He says this, "*Put me in remembrance; let us argue together; set forth your case, that you may be proved right" (43:26)*. Throughout the Bible, many of the chosen men and women of God took advantage of the imperative the LORD makes in the book of Isaiah. It is worth mentioning that as a result of the stand the daughters of Zelophehad took and had their case brought before the LORD, not only did they receive their blessing/inheritance but God provided the resolution to similar cases/laws as theirs (Numbers 27:8-11). I often wondered if the other similar cases would have ever been resolved had those five daughters of Zelophehad not stood up for what they believed was right. Many others were blessed because the daughters knew their rights and had enough courage to bring their case before Moses and ultimately the 'High Court', the Judge. God always has the last *Word*! Of course, that is what transpires when we study the *Logos* and are willing to take a stand not as complaining people of God but people who have *Knowledge* of God's Will, which is in His *Word*. Perhaps, for these reasons, Paul prayed for the church in Colossae that they would be *"Filled with the knowledge of his will in all spiritual wisdom and understanding, to lead a life worthy of the Lord, fully pleasing to him, bearing fruit in every good work and increasing in the knowledge of God" (Colossians 1:9-11)*. We may never KNOW what is in the LORD's Will specifically for us, but we are encouraged to <u>UNDERSTAND</u> and <u>*KNOW*</u> what IS the Will of the LORD. The Apostle Paul warns in his writing to the church in Ephesus of this very thing, *"Therefore do not be foolish, but understand what the will of the LORD is" (Ephesians 5:17)*. This passage would suggest that if we do not <u>UNDERSTAND</u> the LORD's Will, we walk as foolish people. Paul also testifies of the initial purpose of his 'calling' to <u>KNOW</u> the LORD's Will by saying,

> *And at that very hour, I received my sight and saw him. And he said, "The God of our fathers appointed you to know his will to see the Just One and to hear a voice from his mouth; for you will be a witness for him to all men of what you have seen and heard."*
>
> *(Acts 22:13-15)*

When we UNDERSTAND and KNOW the Will of the LORD, He makes us accountable concerning the *Knowledge* of His Will. As Jesus teaches, He says this, *"And that servant who knew his master's will but did not make ready or act according to his will shall receive a severe beating" (Luke 12:47)*. Jesus reminds us of the punishment that would be inflicted on us who have the *Knowledge* and do not act accordingly. Lastly, the LORD desires for us to <u>DO</u> His Will. For Jesus clearly states His assignment in the earth, *"My food is to do the will of God" (John 4:34)*. Surely, we will be unable to <u>DO</u> His Will unless we <u>UNDERSTAND</u> and <u>KNOW</u> it. Likewise, there is no way we the believers will be able to <u>UNDERSTAND</u>, <u>KNOW</u>, and <u>DO</u> the LORD's Will unless we study the *Word* of God to discover what's in His Will.

Another profound way that the LORD speaks is by way of His *Rhema Word*. When we study the *Word* of God *(Logos)* and a passage of Scripture resonates in us, it is the *Rhema Word* that Holy Spirit gives us. It was based on the *Logos*, but the *Word* was quickened in us by the Holy Spirit. While diligently searching for God, I studied the Bible very intensely; and Holy Spirit would constantly reveal the *Rhema Word* in many passages of Scripture I was studying. As Holy Spirit spoke directly to me by way of Scripture, He enabled me to overcome whatever obstacles I was faced with at that moment. Consequently, I gained the strength I needed to 'weather' through the situation. No doubt, I had obtained a *Word* from God Himself; and it was my *Rhema Word*. However, there is another more excellent way in which God speaks His *Rhema* for the purpose of our *KNOW*. For example, many years ago as I was driving through a neighborhood in my city, the LORD spoke these words to me very clearly, "We Are Conquerors". My mind quickly recalled the passage of Scripture (the *Logos*), which the Apostle Paul wrote that says, *"Nay, in all these things we are more than conquerors through him who love us" (Romans 8:37)*. I believed those words when I read them; however, because the LORD spoke those words directly to me, it became my *Rhema*. Now, I *KNOW* it; and I walk in the *Power* of it. In the book of Genesis God had spoken to Jacob, the son of Isaac, given him instructions, and made great promises to him prior to his encounter with a potential angry brother named Esau, from whom he had stolen his birthright. This is what the LORD had promised Jacob in His initial meeting with him,

> *I am the LORD, the God of Abraham your father and the God of Isaac; the land on which you lie I will give to you and to your descendants…Behold, I am with you and will keep you wherever you go, and will bring you back to this land; for I will not leave you until I have done that of which I have spoken to you.*
>
> *(Genesis 28:13-15)*

Because the LORD had spoken to Jacob's *KNOW* prior to his brother's coming to meet him, while he was fraught with fear, he stood on the *Rhema Word*. He put the LORD in remembrance as he spoke these words,

> *O God of my father Abraham, and God of my father Isaac, the LORD which saidst unto me, Return unto thy country, and to thy kindred, and I will deal well with thee: I am not worthy of the least of all the mercies, and of all the truth, which thou hast shewed unto thy servant, for with my staff I passed over this Jordan; and now I am become two bands. Deliver me, I pray thee, from the hand of my brother, from the hand of Esau; for I fear him, lest he will come and smite me, and the mother with the children.*
>
> *(Genesis 32:9-11)*

The *'Tell'* of Two Voices

Even though Jacob was fearful of death from the hand of Esau, he knew that he had heard from God because God had given him the *Rhema Word*, that which was spoken directly out of God's mouth. Consequently, it became his *KNOW*. He quickly reminded God of what He had told him,

> *But thou didst say, 'I will do you good, and make your descendants as the sand of the sea, which cannot be numbered for multitude.'*
>
> *(Genesis 32:12)*

It is the *Rhema* that God speaks directly to an individual that causes one to *KNOW*. That, of course, emanates from being in His manifest Presence. In my personal experience with the Master while receiving the *Rhema Word*, the Holy Spirit allows me not only to remember what He *tells* me, but where I was when He said it and exactly what He said. Because I am a habitual writer of the *Rhema Word* daily, I record dates; and I occasionally revisit the words the LORD speaks. Although I remind Him of His written Word *(Logos)* through Scripture, the *Rhema* Word gives me a greater assurance and strengthens my faith because it comes directly from His mouth. The Presence of the LORD is the place where the LORD begins to speak His *Rhema*. That is in 'clear', not 'dark speech'. It is important to note that many believers who are unable to hear or discern the LORD's Voice will question if others, who have the *Rhema*, are hearing from God. When Moses' sister Miriam and his brother Aaron criticized him behind his back for his selection of his significant other, the LORD sets the record straight on how He views Moses, particularly in the way He communicates with him. He says this,

THE POWER OF KNOW

Listen to my words: 'When a prophet of the LORD is among you, I reveal myself to him in visions, I speak to him in dreams. But not so with my servant Moses; he is faithful over my whole house. With him I speak mouth to mouth, clearly, and not in dark speech; he sees the form of the LORD'.

(Numbers 12:6-8)

The LORD revealed to Moses' siblings this one thing—that which Moses speaks and hears from Him is KNOW because He has Rhema, 'clear language' from His Mouth.

I re-emphasize the fact that people have the tendency to doubt the 'real Truth' that the Holy Spirit speaks to certain individuals. In the body of Christ, sometimes there is a false perception of how people hear from God. People must 'look' and 'talk' anointed or be of a certain stature in order for anything that comes out of their mouths to be taken seriously. The Apostle Paul was faced with a similar scenario while traveling on a ship with prisoners. Paul advised the centurion who was in charge of the prisoners that they would have a tempestuous voyage out on the sea if they set sail. Apparently, Paul was perceived as 'insignificant'; so the centurion took the advice of the captain and the ship's owner in lieu of his. People will rather receive ungodly counsel from another than to accept the wisdom of God. Oftentimes they jettison God's wisdom/counsel and count it as foolishness. The LORD reminds us in His Word that even His foolishness is counted wiser than men (I Corinthians 1:25). After the ship became wrecked, Paul says this, *"Men you should have listened to me and should not have set sail from Crete and incurred this injury*

The 'Tell' of Two Voices

and loss" (Acts 27:21). The consequence of the captain and the ship owner's decision was so detrimental that it could have led to death had it not been for the intervention of the Almighty God who saved them and the *Rhema Word* Paul had received from God. Now, Paul releases the Rhema,

> *For this very night, there stood by me an angel of the LORD to whom I belong and whom I worship and he said, 'Do not be afraid, Paul. You must stand before Caesar; and lo, God has granted you all those who sail with you. So take heart, men, for I have faith in God that it will be exactly as I have been told.*
> (Acts 27:23-26)

The words, *'it will be exactly as I have been told',* echoes "The LORD Told Me". That was Paul's *Rhema*, his *KNOW*—that which emanated directly from the mouth of God. As a result of the *Rhema*, Paul was able to encourage the men who obviously saw him in a different way now than before. Because of the *Power of KNOW—The Word* from God Himself, which Paul released, they all had a safe landing (Acts 27: 44).

The question remains, "Who will you believe—the flesh or the Spirit of Truth?" Even though *The 'Tell' of Two Voices* specifically reveals that the *Logos* is for our <u>belief</u>, it clearly solidifies that the *Rhema* is for our *KNOW*. Both are powerful and serve as a reminder that we have a God who keeps His *Word* and desires His people to be drawn closer to Him that we may *Believe* and ultimately *KNOW* Him. What God says to us, He is able to perform it exactly the way He says it. *KNOW* in the *Word* of God is important to the believer's Faith. And it has *Power!*

PART III

In The *Worship*

CHAPTER 11
The *'Tell'* of Two *'Wells'*

Not only does our *KNOW* have *Power* in the *Word*, but it has *Power* in our *Worship*. Living in the LORD's manifest Presence, I have discovered that the LORD *'tells'* for a purpose. That purpose is to bring change in the believer's overall experience with Him; and if nothing else, it enables His people to become knowledgeable of who He is. That *Knowledge* causes one to grow in Grace, transitioning from the 'milk' to eating 'solid food' as the Apostle Paul references in letters he wrote to the church at Corinth (I Corinthians 3:1-3). The LORD also *'tells'* so that we might become *True Worshipers* and, ultimately, *'tell'* a crooked, dying world about Jesus Christ, our LORD and Savior. As I pen these words, I am reminded of two ladies, Rebecca (Genesis 24:15-28) and the Samaritan woman (John 4:7-29), in the Old and New Testaments, who made visits to *wells* to draw water. As I compared and contrast the two, I discovered that something was unique that stemmed from their visits. Although in separate generations, each encountered men in her visit; and both ran to *'tell'*. Even though they were not looking nor expecting anything from the *'well'* but to draw water, neither of the two women left empty-handed. They each left with something different from their visits. Rebecca met a servant who brought news that she was chosen to be the wife of the son of the patriarch Abraham. She did not realize that she would eventually become the wife of Isaac who would birth a son (Jacob) who would father the 12 tribes/sons of Israel. The Samaritan woman's meeting was totally different from her predecessor's. She did not meet just a man but the Messiah, Jesus Christ Himself. She not only found the Savior, but she had the honor and privilege of sitting and dining with Him as He ministered to her. For Jesus spoke Truth to her inner being. He spoke to her *KNOW.* As mentioned in a previous chapter, the LORD seeks to minister to our inward being, and such occurs in a divine meeting with Him. It is worth noting that it is also the place where CHANGE occurs. The Samaritan woman received something more precious than Rebecca, who received a husband. She received her ministry, healing, deliverance, Truth, and best of all the Husband of husbands, Jesus. More than anything, she became knowledgeable of how the LORD defines a *True Worshiper.* As Jesus interacted with her and even corrected her, He spoke these words,

> *Woman, believe me, the hour is coming when neither on this mountain nor in Jerusalem will you worship the Father. You worship what you do not know; we worship what we know, for salvation is from the Jews. But the hour is coming, and is now here, when the true worshipers will worship the Father in spirit and truth, for the Father is seeking such people to worship him.*
>
> *(John 4:21-23)*

It is clear from the above passage when Jesus speaks these words—*You worship what you do not know; we worship what we know*—that God is looking for people who will *worship* Him because they *KNOW* Him. Primarily, that includes what He personally speaks to them. In our place of *worship* and other chosen places, people are worshiping the LORD but the question that comes to mind is this, "Is it in Spirit and Truth?"

The 'Tell' of Two 'Wells'

That is the type of *worship* which the LORD desires, for He has defined it. He desires it to the point that He diligently seeks the worshipers. In other words, the LORD searches or looks for them. Because He wants His people to *KNOW* Him, in order to get the *worship* out of them that He deserves, He MAKES them into the *True Worshiper*. After all, how can we truthfully tell someone about him or herself unless we *KNOW* him or her. Of course, that includes spending invaluable time with the individual. It is virtually impossible to *KNOW* God from a distance. Consequently, we will be unable **authentically** to *tell* Him who He is. We MUST come close so that the Holy Spirit can *'tell'* us. Otherwise, what we say might become flattery. The LORD does not want flattery from His people! In several passages in the Word of God, we are reminded of the dangers of flattery. Solomon writes this in the book of Proverbs, *"A person who flatters his neighbor is spreading a net for him to step into..." (29:5)*. In a previous Scripture he writes, *"A lying tongue hates those it hurts, and a flattering mouth works ruin" (26:28)*. *"In the end, people appreciate honest criticism far more than flattery" (28:23)*. Paul gives reason for refraining from flattery when he says this in his letter to the church at Thessalonica, *"For we never used flattering speech, as you know, or had greedy motives. God is our witness and we didn't seek glory from people, either from you or from others" (I Thessalonians 2:5-6)*. There are a host of other Scriptures that speak of the dangers of using flattery. In the book of Psalms, David describes how unfaithful the children of Israel were to God on their journey out of Egypt to the Promise Land, *"Nevertheless they flattered him with their mouth, and they lied unto him with their tongues. For their heart was not right with him, neither were they steadfast* *in his covenant" (78:36-37).* These were God's people who constantly lied to Him. The question is this, "If when we flatter people with untruths and we are told how detrimental it is to us, then how much more do we think it would be to God?" Not only are there consequences, but our *worship* becomes feign. For these reasons alone, it is imperative that we get into His manifest Presence and allow Him to *'tell'* us, as He did Moses, David, Herstine, and so many others, who He really is—the *Words* which speaks to our *KNOW.* Daily, the LORD stands ready to constantly *'tell'* us who He is. As He *'tells',* we *'retell'.* In other words, as He *'tells'* us that He is Great, Wonderful, Worthy, Excellent, Powerful, Good, etc., we *'tell'* Him back! All the accolades He reveals about Himself, *'Tell Him Back!'*

Like the Samaritan woman, the LORD's intent is to bring All to the *'well'* and give All a drink of the Living Water. There is no need to set an appointment; He still awaits at the *'well'* daily for that thirsty soul. More than anything, we will discover that it is the place where we have a Divine Encounter with the Master and leave with a *KNOW.* That way, we give Him 'real *Worship'*— that which He deserves and what He created us to do. With that *Knowledge,* we too can join in with the Samaritan woman and even Queen Sheba from her visit with King Solomon. Even though Queen Sheba did not visit a *'well'* or have an encounter with the King of kings, she had an unusual visit with a king; and many centuries later she was worthy of Jesus' mentioning her in His teaching when He says this to the onlookers,

> *The queen of Sheba will rise up at the judgment with the men of this generation and condemn them, for she came from the ends of the earth to hear the wisdom of Solomon, and behold, something greater than Solomon is here.*
> *(Luke 11:31)*

The *'Tell'* of Two *'Wells'*

In essence, Jesus is saying to the people with whom He was speaking that if Queen Sheba traveled across the world just to hear the wisdom of a man named Solomon, she would judge the people of this generation and even condemn them because they refused to *KNOW* and reverence who was in their presence, the Savior of the world. She was filled with an 'awe' from the wisdom of a man when she returned to her country, including a report, a *'tell',* that—*"The Half Has Not Been Told"*. Nevertheless, we have an awesome God in our midst daily who desires such a fellowship with His people. As we *Worship* Him, He will give us a report—"What I read and studied", "What I was taught and preached", and "What I heard prophesized," *"The Half Has Not Been Told!"*

No doubt, each woman's (Rebecca and the Samaritan woman) visit to the *'well'* was impactful; and each left with treasures. Out of the womb of Rebecca was the powerful lineage from which Jesus proceeded, the tribe of Judah. The woman of Samaria eventually became a *True Worshiper* because in her Divine Encounter with Jesus, she came to *KNOW* Him. Also, she became a 'trailblazer' for the *'well'* of God by reminding us that there is still room; and when we sit and dine with the Master, we will indeed possess *KNOW* Power, thus causing us to give the LORD 'real *Worship*'. When we possess *KNOW* Power, we too will testify that, "We were led to the *'well'* to be delivered from *'hell',* and we were made *'well'* so we could *'tell'*!" When we get into the Presence of the Almighty King and allow Him to speak to our *KNOW,* not only will we *'tell'* Him who He is daily as we *Worship* Him, but *'tell'* the world that we have found the Savior and "He Is Sweet Because **I** *KNOW*."

CHAPTER 12
HAIL! Prevails Against Hell

The LORD desires us to become *True Worshipers* not only to give Him His due, but He wants us to *KNOW* that there is *Power* in our *Worship*. And that *Power* is manifest when we become *True Worshipers*. Let me parenthetically say that *Worship* is non-negotiable. It is not contingent upon what God will give or do for us in exchange for reverence to Him. Absalom, the son of David, had an evil agenda when he negotiated with God. Before he returned from exile to the city of Jerusalem where he had been barred by his father for murdering his brother, Amnon, and in his subterranean plot to remove his father David from his throne, he made a vow to the LORD with these words, *"If the LORD will indeed bring me back to Jerusalem, then I will worship the LORD"* (2 Samuel 15:8). Not only did Absalom have the wrong motive and perception of *Worship,* but these words paint a vivid picture of how some believers may view *Worship* today. We do not tell the LORD that "If you do this or that for me, then I will *Worship* you." As children of the Most High God, we should be committed and determined to *Worship* our King without expecting to receive anything from Him in return. The LORD deserves it, and it belongs to Him!

As I was seeking the LORD many years ago and even getting into His Presence, the LORD spoke these words, *"A Higher Call To Worship Another Level Of Praise That I Am Calling You To".* The Holy Spirit was telling me that I was at a level of praising and worshiping Him, but He wanted to take me to another level. He wanted more; He wanted me to become a *True Worshiper.* As prefaced in the previous chapter, the LORD had to MAKE me into one. I did not know how to be a *True Worshiper* until I got into His Presence; and that was not done overnight. I had to constantly pray and study the Word of God as I praised and sought the LORD daily to develop a kinship with Him. All was done for the purpose of KNOWING Him. Hence, I can rightly say that not only did I learn how to *Worship* but the *Power* in *Worship*; and that was only from growing in the manifest Presence of the LORD. I also learned just how important *Worship* is to the LORD and the methods He uses to make us into *True Worshipers.*

Mary and Mary Magdalene, the women who rushed to the tomb of Jesus after He had risen from the grave, eagerly became worshipers after they experienced something very amazing about Jesus. This is what Scripture says that happened to them,

> *So they departed quickly from the tomb with fear and great joy, and ran to tell his disciples. And behold, Jesus met them and said, "Hail!" And they came up and took hold of his feet and worshiped him.*
> *(Matthew 28:8-9)*

The above passage gives us insight into the mighty greeting of God, *"Hail!" "Hail!"* is a powerful salute or greeting. As a matter of fact, I believe that when Jesus accosted the women with the greeting of *"Hail!"*, it was spoken with so much intensity and power that an aroma of the Lord's Presence was released.

The women were so ecstatic that they were compelled to come close, cleave to Jesus' feet, and *Worship* Him. For one, they KNEW who He was.

God wants to meet and greet each of us daily with a *"Hail!"* in His own Supernatural way. Of course, his happens when we come before His Throne to seek His Face, i.e, to pray, give thanks, and *Worship* Him. I am a witness that He does. Often times when I get down on my knees to pray and *worship* the King, His Presence engulfs me with a *"Hail!"*, that puissant greeting, assuring me that He is right there listening and ready to receive my offering. That *"Hail!"* is not an audible Voice; it is His Presence as He grabs a hold of me. Like Mary and Mary Magdalene, I am compelled to give Him His due, *True Worship*. Let me parenthetically say that the LORD does not greet us only during prayer but occasionally throughout the day when we are not praying. However many times the LORD visits us with a *"Hail!"* in a given a day, we should *Worship* Him and bless His Name! If we are shopping, working, doing routine chores, and feel His Glorious Presence, the LORD's *"Hail!"*, *Worship* Him! We do not have to make a scene in public, but we can bless His Name in our own private way. Whether at home or in the streets, I find myself blessing His Name throughout the day because He constantly visits me with a *"Hail!"* While the Apostle John was a prisoner on the island of Patmos, the LORD revealed the Supernatural things of heaven to Him. The angel instructed him to write about how blessed God's people are and who would be invited to the wedding feast of the Lamb of God. John was so overwhelmed by this heavenly experience that he fell at the feet of the angel to *Worship* him. However, the angel responds, *"You must not do that! I am a fellow servant with you and your brothers the prophets, who hold to the testimony of Jesus. Worship God!" (Revelations 22:9).* The angel tells John not to be in awe of him because he was no better than he. He, John, and the others had something in common. They carried the powerful testimony of Jesus! The angel causes John to take the focus off him. He also reminds John that *Worship* does not belong to men. He then instructs John to give God what belongs to Him and Him only. In an urgent and exclamatory way, he tells John to *Worship* the LORD! If the body of Christ would heed to the word that the angel released to John, people would avoid worshiping people who exemplify gifts and popularity in the Household of Faith.

The LORD is interested in meeting all of us with a *"Hail!"* After all, the prophet Isaiah declares, *"Thou meetest him that joyfully works righteousness, those that remember thee in thy ways" (Isaiah 64:5).* The LORD patiently waits to meet with His children who **work** the things which are close to His heart—*Righteous*—and to do it with joy, never forgetting who He is and above all, those who will *Worship* Him. If we have been blessed to have the Great God, the LORD Himself, welcoming us to a meeting with Him, *Worship* Him! For the LORD would have us to *KNOW* that there is *Power* in our *Worship.* Unfortunately, the devil knows it too. The aroma that emits from the LORD's Presence is destructive to the devil's stronghold; and it precludes the gates of hell from prevailing against us. The *Power* in our *Worship* sets the atmosphere in our homes, workplace, gyms, church, malls and various places we so often frequent. In the book *FIRESTARTERS! God's FIREmen,* I penned a testimony of what the LORD had revealed to me about the *Power of Worship.* After worshiping the LORD, I would often 'prayer walk' in my neighborhood. Because His Spirit rested upon me, He showed me how powerful His anointing/FIRE was as it was being released in my community through a simple 'prayer walk'. From that experience, I was fully persuaded that damage was done to the devil's Kingdom! Having that revelation, and gaining that Knowledge, I am thoroughly convinced of the *Power* of *KNOW* in our *Worship* and that *Hail! Prevails Against The Gates Of Hell!*

CHAPTER 13
Never Again!
The *Aroma* That Erases

As we posture ourselves to *Worship* the LORD and to have a better understanding of its significance, we will be able to see more clearly the *Power* in it when we *KNOW* God. *Knowing* God takes our *Worship* to new levels and dimensions. We have discussed how the *Power* of our *Worship* sets the atmosphere as it releases a sweet aroma of God everywhere and how that aroma is destructive to the enemy. As we render to the LORD what's pleasing to Him, we are giving Him what belongs to Him. The *Power* of 'real *Worship*' can also change the mind of God. For instance, the patriarch Abraham was able to change the LORD's mind by literally negotiating with Him. He was such a friend of God and so highly regarded by Him that in his negotiating, he was able to convince the LORD to preserve his nephew Lot, who had moved to Sodom, from the death and destruction that was coming upon it (Genesis 18:16-33). It is good to *KNOW* that we have a God who is so faithful that He is willing to have a conversation with the believers and listen to what we have to say as He graciously accepts the case we plead before Him. Perhaps, that is why He encourages us in the book of Isaiah to reason with Him (Isaiah 1:18). There are many passages of Scripture that are relevant to the LORD's intervention into the lives of His people, especially His chosen. Indeed, the LORD is willing to listen to our hearts and even reason with us. After all, He is a God of equity. However, what captured my attention was the actions of Noah. Noah was able to avert an anathema that was about to be placed upon the 'new world' after God had destroyed the previous world in the flood. If the curse had not been averted, we would have had to endure the ramifications of what God had originally intended to do in the Earth. However, Noah lifted up an aroma to the LORD that was so profound that this is what happened,

> *The LORD smelled the soothing aroma; and the LORD said to Himself, 'I will never again curse the ground on account of man, for the intent of man's heart is evil from his youth; and I will never again destroy every living thing, as I have done.'*
>
> (Genesis 8:21)

After studying the aforementioned passage, we can conclude that our *Worship* has great influence and *Power* to change the mind of the Great King. 'Real *Worship*' can touch the LORD's heart to the extent that whatever His original intent was, it can be reversed and averted. Instead of being cursed, we are blessed; and we enjoy the blessings God has intended for us, His children. If we, the people of God, would release a pleasing odor into the nostril of God daily, God will preserve us and reverse some things that were destined to happen to us because of our disobedience and sinful ways. Our *KNOW*, indeed, has *Power*; and that *Power* is manifest in our *Worship*.

Never Again! The *Aroma* That Erases

Since we are receiving a Kingdom that is unshakable, let us be thankful and please God by worshiping him with holy fear and awe.

(Hebrews 12:28)

CHAPTER 14
Knowledge of His Glory

Being in the manifest Presence of God, I have discovered that the LORD desires His people to come into a kinship with Him like we have never known before. For one thing, He wants to reveal Himself. As we become *True Worshipers* and *KNOW* the *Power* in our *Worship*, the LORD will do just that—reveal Himself. So many believers are still viewing Him from a distance, and they see Him as latent. However, if the truth be told, He desires for His people to come closer so that He may show them that He is not a 'hidden' God. Yes, He remains dormant or 'hidden' until we search Him out. In other words, He wants to be found by His people. In Chapter 1, I stated that 'finding' God is the main purpose of mankind. When we find the LORD, we see Him and we walk in TRUTH. In a passage of Scripture, it is stated that as surely as He exists, the earth will be filled with the glory of God (Numbers 14:21). As a matter of fact, He wants His *Glory* to dwell in the Earth continually. This is what David writes in Psalms, *"Surely his salvation is for those who fear him that glory may dwell in the land" (Psalms 85:9)*. It is without saying that God desires His *Glory* to fill the Earth. As believers, we should be walking with the Glory in us. As a matter of fact, that is one of the ways the LORD fills the Earth with His *Glory*. We become carriers when we reverence the LORD. Again, He reiterates those words in the book of Habakkuk, *"For the earth shall be filled with the knowledge of the glory of God as the waters cover the sea" (2:14)*. We see clearly that it is God's desire to replete the Earth not only with His Glory but with the *Knowledge* of it. According to the Apostle Paul, it is the Truth that enables us to obtain the *Glory* of our LORD Jesus Christ" *(2 Thessalonians 2:13-14)*. The LORD knows when we become knowledgeable of His *Glory*, we automatically have *Knowledge* of Him as we seek more of Him. *Knowledge* of His *Glory* assures us that we are connected to Divinity in a powerful way—that we truly serve a Holy, Magnificent, Supernatural, Incredible, Awesome, and Amazing God. As humans, it also reveals how futile we are and how dependent we are upon His Greatness. The precursor to *Knowledge* is the *Glory* of God. When the angel of the LORD appeared to the shepherds to bring good news of the birth of Jesus, this is what happened,

> *...and the glory of the LORD shone around them, and they were filled with fear. And the angel said to them, "Be not afraid; for behold, I bring you good news of a great joy which will come to all the people; for to you is born this day in the city of David a Savior, who is Christ the LORD".*
> *(Luke 2:9-11)*

Needless to say, the shepherds were in awe after witnessing a powerful presentation of heaven, and, of course, having their own Supernatural experience in the *Glory* of God. They heard the angels in heaven singing and praising God. However, the shepherds did not just bask in the thrill of it all. After the angel who brought the tidings left them and returned to heaven, they did something. They decided to *KNOW* more—seek the Christ. Not only does the revelation of the *Glory* of God and experiencing a touch of His *Glory* prepare us to receive *Knowledge*, it prepares us to seek *Knowledge*. The shepherds decided to look for what had been revealed to them. *"Let us go over to Bethlehem and see this thing that has happened, which the LORD has made known to us" (Luke 2:15).* Having an encounter with Divinity/the *Glory* of God prepared them to seek and to find what had already been *told* them by the angel. Experiencing the *Glory* of God will cause one to want more and more of the LORD. *"And when they saw it, they made known the saying, which had been told them, concerning the child, and all who heard it wondered at what the shepherds told them" (Luke 2:17).* Not only did the shepherds find the Savior, but they made Him KNOWN. Indeed, having a Divine experience is something one cannot keep to himself nor be reticent. Moreover, *Knowledge* of His *Glory* comes with a higher expectation and accountability. When the LORD shows us His *Glory*, it will mature us, strengthen our faith, and make us knowledgeable of Him. He expects us to give Him more of our time, talents, energy, treasures, and, of course, *Worship* Him even the more.

Seeing His Glory/FIREworks

God did not cause only the shepherds and others in the Bible to have a heavenly, Supernatural experience but His people today as well. Mankind, whether they admit it or not, innately crave the Supernatural, primarily because we are Supernatural creatures having a natural experience. Being cognizant of this very fact, the arts and entertainment world has inundated society with television shows and movies depicting a false Supernatural. From childhood to adulthood, we see and have been shown movies and television episodes of superheroes such as Mighty Mouse, Superman, Batman, Spiderman, Wonder Woman, Black Panther, Avengers, and a host of others. Seeing the LORD's *Glory* gives us a view of the Supernatural God. A great part of that is to see His *FIREworks*. We see a superficial presentation of *FIREworks* displayed in various places in our nation on Independence Day/Fourth of July, at sporting and political events, and various other celebrations. The concept of *Fireworks*, no doubt, emanates from the Bible. Man wanted to mimic what God had originally demonstrated. Again, it is an indication of humankind's need and desire to see the Supernatural God, unaware that God has real *Glory/FIREworks* He desires to reveal. Occasionally, He gives the world a cursory look at His *FIREworks* through the lens of the solar eclipse. In a certain year on planet Earth, many travel throughout various parts of the country and wait patiently to see how the Sun, Moon, and Earth are aligned. I have deemed these a heavenly presentation of nature—the things God created. After this powerful presentation of the LORD's display of *Fireworks,* many leave with tears because they are in awe of what they witnessed. However, the LORD's earnest desire is to show His people His *Glory/FIREworks* daily. We enjoy these benefits continually when we live in His manifest Presence and *Worship* Him. Experiencing His *Glory/FIREworks* is an added bonus! In the book of Leviticus, Moses tells the people of God what He commands them to do and the manner in which He would 'back-up' His promise if they obeyed Him. He says this, *"This is the thing which the LORD commanded that ye should do: and the glory of the LORD shall appear unto you" (9:6).* God had promised the Israelites a *Glory/FIREworks* show. They were also told what they had to do in order to see it. After they followed Moses' instructions, this is what happened,

And Moses and Aaron went into the tabernacle of meeting, and came out and blessed the people. Then the glory of the LORD appeared to all the people, and fire came out from before the LORD and consumed the burnt offering and the fat on the altar.
(Leviticus 9:23-24)

The LORD kept His Word to the children of Israel by revealing His *Glory* and displaying His *FIREworks!* After His Mighty *FIREworks* presentation, they were so excited and elated by this Supernatural event that they worshiped Him. *"When all the people saw it, they shouted and fell on their faces" (24).* God's presentation of His *FIREworks* always bring excitement and a new level of understanding and awesomeness about Him that we are constrained to *Worship* Him and bless His Name. As stated in a previous chapter, when God reveals Himself in that way, we do not have to make a public scene. Whenever and however the FIRE kindles and ignites in us, we bless His Name as we praise and *Worship* Him. As the children of Israel obeyed Moses' instructions, the LORD rendered to them that which He promised. We plainly see how significant obedience is in the revelation of *His Glory.* When we walk in obedience to the Word of God, the LORD will show Himself in a Supernatural way by showing us the things we have never seen before. He will also release

Supernatural blessings to us in so many difference ways. As the LORD continually reveals Himself to us individually in His Supernatural way, God expects more from us. We are obligated to give Him more and more of His due—*WORSHIP* and the *Glory*. Above all, our *KNOW* is being increased; and the more we *KNOW*, the more we *Worship*! Also, as we see His *Glory/FIREworks* on display, we would be better able to <u>authentically speak</u> of His *Glory*. When the prophet Isaiah was privileged to get a glimpse of the Supernatural in the Throne Room of God in Heaven, He told the awesome things about the LORD that he had witnessed. Jesus gives this account as He speaks about Isaiah to a group of onlookers, *"Isaiah said these things because he saw his glory and spoke of him" (John 12:41)*. We may never have the experience that Isaiah had. However, when God gives us a glimpse of His *Glory/FIREworks* in His own special way, primarily on the inside of us, we will speak only of what He allows us to witness.

It is imperative that we remember that as the LORD takes us to unusual 'eye hath not seen nor ear heard' places, we do not become prideful and attempt to 'steal' His *Glory*. It is important to note that when Isaiah saw His *Glory* and spoke of Him, he did not see, speak, and **take** His *Glory* as many do. The LORD has proven in Scripture what destructive things can happen when people do such. All the *Glory* truly belongs to the LORD, so every effort should be made by His people to give Him what belongs to Him. In the book of Leviticus, Aaron's two sons, Nadab and Abihu, who were also anointed priests, were destroyed because they attempted to 'steal' the LORD's *Glory*. After they witnessed the LORD's Holy *FIREworks* in the presence of Moses and the people, they decided to get

Glory for themselves and display their *Fireworks*. They took a censer and put fire in it along with incense and burned it before the LORD with the hope of being glorified perhaps in the sight of the people. Their fire was unholy or strange to God, though. Unfortunately, by offering 'unholy fire' before God, they both were destroyed by FIRE (Leviticus 10:10). The LORD reveals His stance in the matter by saying, *"I will be sanctified in them that come nigh me, and before all the people I will be glorified" (10:3).* There is no man's *Fire* that can be compared to God's—NONE! Consequently, there should be no competition! God has blessed people all over the world with special gifts, talents, abilities, intellect, skills, ideas, etc. Many have obtained wealth and prosperity, but they refuse to give Him *Glory.* That is clearly an example of stealth. They take all the accolades, strokes, 'pats-on-the-back', without ever giving the LORD thanks and above all, the *Glory!* He expects it from the unbeliever as well as the believer. In the book of Acts, God killed king Herod for refusing to give Him *Glory.* After the people praised Herod for an extraordinary public address he made and even acknowledged that it was the voice of a god and not of a man, this is what happened next, *"And immediately, because Herod did not give glory to God, an angel of the LORD struck him down, and he was eaten by worms and died" (Acts 12:23).* It was Herod's responsibility to intervene and say, "No, don't praise a god; it was the Great God that enabled me to say these words, Praise HIM, Give *Glory* to God!" He, however, allowed a god to get the *Glory* and failed to give it to the Almighty God. Moreover, Moses could not enter the Promise Land because he did not reverence God as holy in the midst of His people at the waters of

Meribah. In other words, he did not allow God to present His Supernatural show.

> *Then Moses and Aaron went from the presence of the assembly to the entrance of the tent of meeting and fell on their faces. And the glory of the LORD appeared to them, and the LORD spoke to Moses, saying, "Take the staff, and assemble the congregation, you and Aaron your brother and tell the rock before their eyes to yield its water. So you shall bring water out of the rock for them and give drink to the congregation and their cattle."*
>
> (Numbers 20:6-8)

Moses apparently was disgusted with the congregation for their unbelief and continual complaints. Furthermore, he had probably grown weary of having to constantly intercede for the people to preclude God's wrath from destroying them as he stood in the gap for them. Even though God had given clear instructions to Moses, this is what happened, *"And Moses lifted up his hand and struck the rock with his staff twice, and water came out abundantly, and the congregation drank, and their livestock" (Numbers 20:11)*. Moses, who had previously proven Himself to be faithful, made a terrible mistake. For his anger and frustration and his failure to follow the instructions God had given him, he prevented the LORD from receiving the *Glory* He wanted in the midst of His people. He failed to reverence the LORD as Holy. It also appeared that he had embarrassed God before His people when he failed to do what he was instructed to do. Although we cannot compare God's feelings or actions with man's, many of us abhor being embarrassed in the presence of others. If someone has to utter any disparaging words to us, we would prefer they pull us to the side and speak. Unfortunately, in many situations, that is not the case. People, with the obvious intent of belittling and embarrassing another, will wait for that opportune moment to blur out in the presence of others that very thing they should not speak. I am sure that it was not Moses' intent to do such. He loved God's people and he had proven that. However, that was the manner in which it appeared. For the LORD desires His people to See HIM! It is clear that our attitude, disobedience, and failure to follow the LORD's instructions play significant roles in not allowing the LORD to show Himself Strong and Mighty and Holy in the presence of His people. We can conclude that the LORD desires to be glorified in all situations and circumstances, especially in the midst of His people. As mentioned in this chapter and a previous chapter, many people have made terrible mistakes for not doing so and have been destroyed.

More than anything, the LORD desires His people to *See* His *Glory/FIREworks* that He **Himself** is able to perform. Consequently, we will *KNOW* that He alone is God; and there is none other who can compare with Him. With that *Knowledge*, our *Worship* becomes acceptable to Him as we render to Him that offering by FIRE, the pleasing odor to the LORD. Also, we are mindful that we cannot produce our own *FIREworks*. The LORD carries the 'match'. It is He who ignites, starts, and kindles the FIRE in us. The LORD is willing and ready to give us that *Glory/FIREworks* show that many long for. He wants to take us from the 'superficial show' to the Supernatural show. I can truly testify as one whom He baptized with His burning

FIRE, I enjoy His *FIREworks* inside of me daily. It causes me great excitement, joy, awe, and above all, reverence to Him. As a result, I return a FIRE offering of *Worship* to Him. It is important to note that when we give the LORD an offering of FIRE, we are giving Him His bread or food (Leviticus 21:6,8), making it a pleasing odor to the LORD. However, as the LORD reveals His *Glory/FIREworks,* we *Worship* Him even the more. More than anything, <u>**KNOW**</u> that all the *Glory* belongs to Him!

PART IV

In The *Works*

CHAPTER 15
FIRST Works

As discussed in previous sections of the *Power of KNOW* in the *Word* and in the *Worship*, it is worth mentioning that our *KNOW* has *Power* in the *Works.* The *Works* play a significant role in the overall purpose of this dynamic trio. When we *KNOW* God, we will be determined to obey His *Word*, become a *True Worshiper*, and, of course, do His *Works*. Indeed, the *Knowledge* of God causes believers to do Great *Works* for the Kingdom. Plainly speaking, our *KNOW* is for Him to be *KNOWN*. The more God reveals Himself to us the more we should be compelled to make Him *KNOWN* in the Earth. It is important that we realize that *Works* is not defined as a physical performance alone. It is rather a mindset determined to serve the LORD regardless of any situation because He has revealed Himself in such an incredible way, which makes us *KNOW* Him in an awesome way. None of our performances impress God if we do not LOVE Him with all of our heart, mind, soul, and strength (Matthew 22:37), (Mark 12:30), (Luke 10:27), (Deuteronomy 6:5). If we are not in a close kinship with God, the *Works* we perform in the Earth will prove to be irrelevant. Being in the LORD's Presence daily, I *KNOW* with surety that above everything, He wants us to have intimacy with Him—to love Him and to love on Him! Being mindful of this very fact, we should have a definitive understanding and revelation of the *FIRST* Works, which the LORD requires from every believer. The two sisters, Mary and Martha, received a revelation of how God perceives the *FIRST Works* the physical performances. As one complained to Jesus about her physical labor while the other 'hung out' with Him, Jesus set the record straight and clearly articulated His preference, *"But one thing is necessary. Mary has chosen the good portion, which will not be taken away from her" (Luke 10:42).* For the LORD knows that when we are passionate about Him FIRST, we will have a genuine passion for the things/*Works* He is passionate about. His passion then becomes our passion. For these reasons, John was instructed by the Holy Spirit to write letters to the seven churches expressing God's heart and His expectation from the church and its designated leadership. To the first church, the LORD expressly says, *"I know your works...... but this one thing I have against you, you have left your first love; do the first works" (Revelation 2:2-7).* The LORD is displeased with the church or individuals who are not passionate about Him *FIRST,* i.e., loving Him, communing with Him, via prayer, thanksgiving, studying the Word, worshiping and praising Him daily. If we do not make our passion for the LORD our number one priority, any performances/*Works* that we render have no power in their effects. Perhaps, this is why these words are written in the gospel— that our *FIRST Works* is not to go to the streets rashly to win souls for the Kingdom, but to *Believe* (John 6:29). That is the believers' *FIRST* duty. We must *FIRST* believe that the LORD is God and that His Son Jesus is the Christ who died for us that we may be forgiven of our sins and have eternal life. When we do the *FIRST Works*—believe in Him and fall in love with Him, then we will position ourselves to do His *Works.*

FIRST Works

KNOW His Works

As we demonstrate our *FIRST Works* by believing, communing, fellowshipping, and developing a kinship with the LORD, there is another part of the *Works* that He requires of us. As a matter of fact, our *FIRST Works* is not consummated without recognizing a very important component of our love affair with the Master. That component is His *Works*. Not only are we commanded to do His *Works* but to ACKNOWLEDGE His *Works, the things He has done.* Acknowledging the LORD's *Works* is to reverence The Greatness of His Kingdom and what He has done for us. Every individual in this Earth, both young and old, small or great, desires to have his or her deeds/achievements recognized by others. We enjoy the accolades, applauses, 'strokes' when we achieve the things that we feel are worth mentioning. It gives us a sense of worth. Well, the LORD does not need to be given a sense of worth, He is Worth—He Is Worthy! However, He wants His Creation to *KNOW* what kind of GOD they serve—that He is a Compassionate, Merciful, Gracious, Faithful, Good, Great, Strong and Mighty God!! In the book of Job, a passage of Scripture reminds us to, *"Remember to extol his work, of which men have sung" (Job 36:24).* Another passage says this, *"He seals up the hand of every man, that all men may know his work" (Job 37:7).* God is a Great God and worthy of all honor, glory, and praise; and He desires for His people to *KNOW* it! Growing up in a Baptist church and attending many special programs, I would often hear recitations of *The Creation* by James Weldon Johnson, which depicted the things concocted by the hands of God. I was always excited when I heard these performances being powerfully dramatized. However, as I grew in my relationship with the LORD and living in His manifest Presence daily, it wasn't until later that I realized the REAL awesomeness of His *Works*. Moreover, the Spirit of Truth would testify of His *Works* in my inward parts as He glorified the LORD (John 16:14). Now, when I observe NATURE and see everything He has fashioned in the Earth, it amazes me; and I see how Amazing He is! I have concluded that NOBOBY COULD DO THE THINGS HE HAS DONE AND THERE IS NOBOBY LIKE THE LORD! The LORD knows that, but He wants us to *KNOW* it and proclaim it to Him daily. No doubt, we are a part of the LORD's *Works*. The fact that we are moving, breathing, living creatures, human beings that He formed from just dust along with other countless things He has made, says a great deal about the Magnificence of God. A great percentage of the books of Psalms is replete with praises and honor to the LORD for His wonderful *Works*. Psalms 105:1-3 encourages us to *"...make known his deeds among the peoples! Sing to him, sing praises to him, tell of all his wonderful works!"* There are a host of other passages in the Word of God that constantly remind us to see His *Works* and acknowledge the Greatness and Majesty of His Hand/Kingdom! I have heard many testify that "I Have Seen Him Work", and they are great testimonies. The question, however, remains, "If We Have Seen Him Work, Are We Acknowledging *His Works* By Telling HIM As Well As Others?" David says this, *"I have made the LORD God my refuge that I may tell of all thy works"* (Psalms 73:28). We also have an obligation to tell of His *Works* even to our children, *"...that the next generation might know them, the children yet unborn, and arise and tell them to their children, so that they should set their hope in God and not forget the works of God, but keep his commandments"* *(Psalms 78:6-7).* We are reminded to *"Bless the LORD, all his works, in all places of his dominion"* *(Psalms 103:22).* The Psalmist also reminds us of how the LORD views His *Works* by saying, *"May the glory of the LORD endure forever; may the LORD rejoice in his works"* *(104:31).* The LORD is pleased with His *Works.* Hence, He is so pleased that He rejoices in them Himself! Just as He rejoices, He wants His Creation to join Him in rejoicing even the more because we are a great part of His *Works.* The LORD sends a stark warning to those who do not acknowledge His *Works*, by saying, *"Because they do not regard the works of the LORD, or the work of his hands, he will break them down and build them up no more"* *(Psalms 28:5).* It is our duty to KNOW the LORD as we LOVE ON Him, and render to Him due credit for the wonderful, incredible *Works* He has done while we do His *Works!* (Psalms 145:10-12). After all, we were chosen for this reason,

> *But you are a chosen generation, a royal priesthood, a holy nation, God's own people, that you may declare the wonderful deeds of him who called you out of darkness into his marvelous light.*
>
> *(1 Peter 2:9)*

CHAPTER 16
Performing the *Exploits*

As we prioritize the *Works* of the LORD, we are able to position ourselves to <u>DO</u> His Works in the Earth. God has commissioned us to *Perform*! The Apostle Paul reminds us of this very fact by saying, *"The kingdom of God does not consist in talk but in power" (I Corinthians 4:20).* Paul's words clearly reveals that our level of boldness is not by our speech, i.e., teaching, preaching, prophesying, singing, etc., but in demonstration of God's Power—allowing the Holy Spirit inside of us to *Work,* i.e., the laying on hands, walking with the FIRE/Glory inside of us to tear down strongholds of the evil one and bring the change in the Earth that is desperately needed for the advancement of God's Kingdom. Many of us fail to realize who is inside us that is doing the real *Work.* Just our mere presence carrying the *Power* of the Great God enables the LORD to do His *Work.* In the book of Daniel, it states this, *"...but the people who know their God shall be strong, and do great exploits" (11:32).* According to this passage, the people who *KNOW* their God are strong, realizing their strength rests in God's Power. In order to *Perform the Great Exploits* and glorify the LORD, it will be imperative that we *KNOW* God. Our knowledge of God causes us to *Perform* in the Earth the deeds in the manner that He has ordained for us to *Perform.* Moreover, when we *KNOW* God, we become serious about doing His *Works.* We must also remember that as children of the Most High God who have been washed in the Blood of the Lamb, we have been ordained by God for service. In the Old Testament, the Levites, the tribe chosen by God to minister to Him, paid a price to ordain themselves for the service of the LORD. After Moses had returned from receiving the Ten Commandments, there was an outbreak of violence in the camp among the children of Israel. They were worshiping the golden calf which Aaron had made, and they engaged themselves in all kinds of riotous, lustful, and other sinful behaviors. Moses, of course, became angry and released an ultimatum to the people as to whose side they were on. *"Then Moses stood in the gate of the camp and said, 'Who is on the LORD's side? Come to me.' And all the Levites gathered themselves together to him" (Exodus 32:26)*. The Levites agreed that they were on the LORD'S side, but they were unaware of the price they had to pay. After Moses' beckoning call, he instructs the Levites on what their next duty would be. *"And he said to them, 'Thus says the LORD God of Israel, Put your sword on your side each of you, and go to and from gate to gate throughout the camp, and each of you kill his brother and his companion and his neighbor'" (Exodus 32:27)*. If the Levites had possessed prior knowledge of what their task would consist of to prove they were on the LORD's side, they probably would have been loath to take an action as such. Perhaps they had to kill their mothers, fathers, sisters, brothers, wives, husbands, children, cousins, including their friends and neighbors. If we would honestly confess, many of us would have had a difficult time agreeing to kill our parents and other close relatives. No doubt, we would have relented. After this horrendous act of blood shedding by the Levites, Moses says this, *"Today you have ordained yourselves for the service of the LORD, each at*

Performing the *Exploits*

the cost of his son and of his brother, so that he might bestow a blessing upon you this day" (Exodus 32:29). What a price these people of God had to pay to ordain themselves to serve God! Thank God for the Redeemer, Jesus Christ, who paid the price for us through the shedding of His Blood on Calvary's Cross for those who believe that we might be ordained by the LORD Himself for His service. We could not and did not do it. Jesus did it! He ordained and qualified us to serve not just inside the House of God but in the Kingdom of God. He did it so that we might *Perform the Great Exploits.* However, it is only through KNOWING the LORD that these *Great Exploits* will be *Performed.*

> *And he said, "Behold, I am making a covenant. Before all your people I will do marvels, such as have not been created in all the earth or in any nation. And all the people among whom you are shall see the work of the LORD, for it is an awesome thing that I will do with you."*
>
> *(Exodus 34:10)*

Partnering in the Work/"We Are In This Thing Together"

It is important to note that as we avail ourselves for the *Work*, we enter into a *Partnership* with the LORD. God never intended for us to act alone to do any *Work* for Him. For He knows that it will not amount to anything without His intervention. In the first book, *Inheriting His Holy Mountain*, that I penned in 2001, I shared with the readers that we should invite the Holy Spirit to *Partner* with us in prayer above any other 'prayer partners' we might choose. Not only should we extend an invitation to Him to *Partner* with us in prayer, but the LORD has given us a *Partner* in the Holy Spirit to assist us in the mission/*Works* so that it will be accomplished in the manner He has willed it to be. In the aforementioned passage, the LORD emphasizes these words, *"for it is an awesome thing that I will do with you" (Exodus 34:10).* We have a God who has always worked through His people throughout the Old and New Testaments, and He desires to work through us to show His Great Power and Might. Nevertheless, there are many people, I believe, of the household of faith that have convinced themselves that they are the ones who are in charge and in control of the projects/assignments God gives; so they do not invite the LORD's intervention. And yes, the LORD looks for good stewards over the *Works*; but He still wants to be included. On the otherhand, there are some believers who are convinced that they will not do anything. They rely totally upon God to perform, failing to realize that the LORD operates by way of *Partnerships*. We have a role to play as we invite Him to intervene. And when we move, or take a bold step, surrender ourselves totally to His Authority, He participates. God is constantly trying to make us *KNOW* that we are special in His sight, even when we think and sometimes believe we are irrelevant. If we are a believer, the LORD has included us in His *Work*manship, His Great Plan of Salvation. Although we are 'oneness' with Him, many do not view it in that manner. It was apparent in John the Baptist's encounter with Jesus. According to Scripture, the Master came from Galilee to the Jordan to be baptized by John. God had included John in His Plan of Salvation, but he could not see himself 'large' enough or even worthy to *Perform/Partner* in such a great W*ork* with and for Jesus. Scripture says, *"John would have prevented him, saying, "I need to be baptized by you, and do you come to me?" (Matthew 3:14).* Of a truth, we are not 'worthy' to share in anything with this Great and Awesome God. However, we must not reject our role in this great *Partnership* which God has so graciously included us because of what we think individually about ourselves. When we do, there is a potential danger of disrupting the Master's Plan. And yes, Jesus sees us as 'Worth', ones who can 'hang out' with Him or do something great with and for Him in the Earth. Because Jesus precluded John from rejecting such an awesome assignment, this is what Scriptures says, *"But Jesus answered him, "Let it be so now; for thus it is fitting for us to fulfill all righteousness" (Matthew 3:15).* In the passage, Jesus reminds John of how he was included in the *Work* and how significant this particular assignment was in the Kingdom of God, *"it is fitting for us",* not He Himself. In other words, Jesus tells John that "It's not about you but about <u>US</u> working together that this thing may be accomplished— *for us to fulfill all righteousness*—execute, achieve this *Great Work*." After John understands his role in God's Great Plan, the Word says, *"Then he consented" (Matthew 3:15).* He came into agreement with Jesus.

God is God all by Himself and needs no one's help, but our Great God chose us that we might be included and *Partner* with Him in the *Works*. I will confess that every task/assignment the LORD gives me, I have always relinquished my authority and invited the Holy Spirit to intervene and take control. My words are, "We Can Do This". After all, the Word declares through the Apostle Paul that *"I can do all things THROUGH Christ which strengthens me" (Philippians 4:13)*. Holy Spirit graciously accepts His *Partnership* role, and I do my part. I have also discovered that He is overly excited to accept the invitation. Entering into this *Partnership* assures that the *Work* will be accomplished and successful. Neglecting or rejecting His counsel is a guaranteed failure. Including the LORD in the *Work* enables us to *KNOW* the *Power* in it and KNOW that *"We Are In This Thing Together!"* God is awaiting us to avail ourselves that He may *Work* through us to *Perform the Great Exploits.*

CHAPTER 17
Be Ready and *Keep* Ready

What an amazing God we serve who has called and elected us to surrender our will to Him that He may *Perform* His *Works* through us for His Glory. With this *Knowledge*, as believers, we must avail ourselves in every way to show that out of all people in the Earth, God chose us to do a *Work* for Him. However, I personally do not believe that many of His people do not consider it an honor to serve Him. My daily prayer is, "LORD, I Thank You For Even Considering To Use Me". When we come to the *Knowledge*, realization, and revelation of how precious God's *Work* is to Him and if we are being used by Him in any facet of His *Works*, we will *KNOW* that it is an honor and a privilege to be chosen to serve Him. Knowing this very fact, we should give Him thanks. The LORD has always been selective about whom He chooses to serve Him. Everyone could not do it. As mentioned in the preceding chapter, the tribe of Levi was chosen above all the others to come close and minister to Him. No other tribes were privy to this honor. Judah may have been selected to be FIRST in praise, war, etc., but the Levites were appointed to stand in the Presence of the LORD and minister to Him. They did not receive the inheritance which was apportioned to the other tribes. I often wondered how the other tribes may have felt when God specifically chose the Levites over them. Their inheritance or portion was the LORD, and He freely gave them His offerings, the best of everything (Numbers 18:21).

THE POWER OF KNOW

God is looking for people who have surrendered themselves to do His Will and are *Ready* to be used by Him. No doubt, He seeks *Ready* people. Not only does God require that we Be *Ready* but *Keep Ready!* The prophet Ezekiel delivers this message from God's command to His people who were preparing for war by saying, *"Be ready and keep ready, you and all your hosts that are assembled about you, and be a guard for them" (38:7).* When we *Keep Ready*, we are always available, prepared, and equipped for the Master's use. The LORD has always looked for a people that would *Keep Ready* in order to serve His Will. Perhaps, that is why David was singled out as one who did <u>all</u> of the LORD's Will. Paul speaks of him as he explains how God demoted Saul and promoted David. He says this as he speaks to the council, *"And when he had removed him, he raised up David to be their king, of whom he testified and said, 'I have found in David the son of Jesse a man after my heart, who will do all my will'" (Acts 13:22).* David was faithful in the *Works* of God because he was prepared when God called upon him. And he was faithful and obedient until his demise. *"Now when David has served God's counsel in his own generation, he fell asleep..." (Acts 13:36).* David was not only *Ready* to do the *Works* of the LORD, he did **all** of God's *Works*. More importantly, he *Kept Ready* until he died. The Apostle Paul also encourages us by saying,

> *Therefore, my beloved brothers, be ye steadfast, unmovable, always abounding in the work of the LORD, for as much you know that your labor is not in vain in the LORD.*
>
> *(I Corinthians 15:58)*

CHAPTER 18
Zealous

The LORD has, no doubt, called us to be about the *Works* of the Kingdom. Yes, He paid the price for us to be forgiven of our sins and to do Kingdom *Work*—to witness to the lost and change a society that is replete with oppression, bigotry, pride, disobedience, rebellion, sin. As Paul explains the purpose of Jesus' death and resurrection, He writes these words in a letter to Titus, *"He gave himself for us to redeem us from all lawlessness and to purify for Himself a people for his own possession who are zealous for good works"* (2:14). As referenced in a previous chapter, the LORD calls us *His People;* and when we wear His Name, we are blessed! In the latter part of the opening Scripture, it says that the LORD saved, sanctified, and purified us, His People, ultimately for this reason, *"that we would be zealous for good works/deeds".* God wants us to be *zealous* for **Him** in our *Works.* I am afraid too many people have become *zealous* for people. God never asked His people to have a *zeal* for people but instead have a *zeal* for Him. He told us to love, forgive, and do good toward people but to be *zealous* for serving Him. While Saul was king of Israel, he made a terrible mistake when he possessed a *zeal* for the people. In his pugnaciousness to destroy the Gibeonites, he went against a sworn oath. *"Now the people of Gibeonites were not of the people of Israel, but of the remnant of the Amorites; although the people of Israel had sworn to spare them, Saul had sought to slay them in his zeal* *for the people of Israel and Judah" (2 Samuel 21:2).* Joshua and the leaders of the people of Israel had previously sworn before God that they would not destroy the Gibeonites if they agreed to become their servants (Joshua 9:3-27). When Saul became king, he did not honor the oath. Because he was *zealous* for the people of Israel, he put the Gibeonites to death. Saul's actions became a 'thorn in David's flesh' when he became king. As a result, God sent a plague in the form of a famine in their land for three years to express his displeasure. We see clearly the ramifications for having a *zeal* for people. The people in Israel had to suffer through a plague upon their land for Saul's mistake and his *zeal* for the people as he desired to please them. The danger of having a *zeal* for people can cause us to become 'people pleasers' in lieu of God-pleasers.

Believers who are *zealous* about the things of God also take a stand for Him and do His *Works*. God has not called the believers to be spiritual spineless people but people who have a jealousy for Him and who are *zealous*. They are soldiers in His army who will stand for His Cause, KNOWING that it is He who will accomplish the mission as He works through them. Being assured of this word in Isaiah that says, *"The zeal of the LORD of host shall accomplish it" (37:32)*, they are keenly aware that it is not they who are doing the *Works* alone but God. The LORD is the <u>Accomplisher</u> because He is the *Zealous* God, and He blesses a *zealous* solider. David was a *zealous* soldier for the LORD, and he pens these words in the book of Psalms, *"For the zeal for thine house has consumed me and the insults of those who insult thee have fallen on me" (69:9)*. David was so *zealous* for God that he was overwhelmed

Zealous

by the things of God. The things that insulted God insulted him. Likewise, we should be insulted about the things satan is doing in our neighborhoods, cities, nation. It is worth mentioning that the LORD does not want our *Works* alone but for us to be **excited** about doing His *Works!* With this in mind, Paul reminds us in the book of Romans of this very thing, *"Never flag in zeal, be aglow with the Spirit, serve the LORD" (12:11).* We do not avail ourselves for the *Work* of the Kingdom with a drudgery spirit. But rather the LORD wants us to be energetic, possessing a spirit of alacrity that the Almighty God would even choose to use us to do the *Works* of His Kingdom. More than anything, the LORD desires for the believer to have a *zeal* according to *Knowledge.* Many years ago as a very young believer, I had a *zeal* for the LORD; but it was without *Knowledge.* God had given me a servant's heart to bless the less fortunate. In my first Outreach Ministry, I went to a homeless women's shelter to bless the women with needful items. That act of service gave me great joy. Prior to that, I also adopted children from poor nations and sent financial gifts bi-weekly to provide food and other resources for them. I was *zealous* for God, but I was not applying or walking in His Word/Truth in the way that I should have. For one thing, I did now KNOW His Word. However, as I grew in Grace and entered His Presence, now my *zeal* is coupled with *Knowledge* of the LORD; and I am more impactful in ministry because they both work in concert with one another. Now I walk with a clear conscience, and I am even the more *zealous* to serve Him. I believe there are many people in the body of Christ who have a *zeal* for God, but it is not coupled with a *KNOW.* For these reasons, Paul prays this prayer for the Romans,

THE POWER OF KNOW

Brethren, my heart's desire and prayer to God for them is that they may be saved. For I bear them witness that they have a zeal for God, but not according to knowledge. For being ignorant of the righteousness of God, and seeking to establish their own, they did not submit to God's righteousness.

(Romans 10:1-3)

In the above passage, Paul reiterates the fact that just possessing a *zeal* for God with the absence of *Knowledge* amounts to zero. Because the people lacked the *Knowledge* of God, thinking they were saved, they apparently performed according to what they considered righteousness; and they refused to submit to God's. A lack of *Knowledge* has negative consequences, and it is detrimental to the so-called believer. Operating with that mindset likens one to God's people in the book of Judges who did what was right in their eyes because there was no Godly leadership in Israel in those days (Judges 17:6). In the times which we live, we too lack Godly leadership from the heads of our nation. However, in the church of Jesus Christ, we have Godly leadership in the form of pastors, under the guidance of the Holy Spirit. Above all, we have the King of kings, the LORD God Almighty, who is in charge and in control and whom we must look to and answer to. When we fail to *KNOW* God, we establish our own way, beliefs, even kingdom! It is evident by the actions of some members of the household of faith's refusal to submit to becoming knowledgeable of God's Word because it is mirrored in their *zeal* for the *Work* of the Kingdom. To be *zealous* for Good *Works* for the LORD is a great thing to possess. The purpose for Jesus' shedding His blood was *"that He would purify our conscience from dead works to serve the living God" (Hebrews 9:14).* If we are truthful, before many of us came into the *Knowledge* of Truth, we were about the business of 'dead works', performing deeds that had nothing to do with glorifying God. But the LORD 'called' us, saved us, and purified us to be *zealous* for His service. Even when we are 'slow' to serve the LORD, He still claims us because He is a patient and faithful God. However, as His People who have His *Name* written on us, it is our duty to humble and avail ourselves to SERVE HIM with a *ZEAL* coupled with **KNOW**ledge!

CHAPTER 19
Abiding Fruit

We have concluded that *Knowledge* plays a very integral and important role in possessing an **authentic** *zeal* for the LORD. When we are *zealous,* we always keep ourselves positioned and postured for the service of the LORD. If God has chosen us to do the *Works* of His Kingdom, that is undoubtedly a blessing and should not by any means be taken for granted. Hence, we were chosen to glorify Him in our *Works*. "But what exactly is the role of the believer to glorify the LORD?" Simply put, we are to *bear fruit.* We have been saved, sanctified, and filled with the Holy Ghost for the purpose of *bearing fruit* for the Master. That is a high-calling for the believer; and for this reason, Jesus taught the principle of *bearing fruit* so profoundly. After He announces the role of the Father (the vinedresser), Himself (the true vine), and illustrates how the believer is unable to function as a branch outside of the vine, He emphasizes the specific purpose of *bearing fruit.* He says this, *"Every branch in me that does not bear fruit He takes away, and every branch that bears fruit He prunes, that it may bear more fruit" (John 15:1-2).* He continues,

> I am the vine, you are the branches. He who abides in me, and I in Him, bears much fruit...If you abide in Me, and my words abide in you, you will ask what you desire, and it shall be done for you. By this my father is glorified, that you bear much fruit and prove to be my disciples.
>
> *(John 15:5-8)*

Jesus clearly outlines specifically what we, the believer, is required to do to glorify God—*bear much fruit.* In the *bearing of fruit* we also prove that we belong to Him. Paul reminds us to be steadfast, unmovable, always abound in the *Work* of the LORD (I Corinthians 15:58). Apparently, he had the revelation that when we constantly do the *Works* of God, *bear much fruit,* the LORD is constantly being glorified. Even in a season of 'storm' in our lives, the LORD requires us to continue to *bear much fruit* because He knows that it is what enables us to get through the storm. This is what the prophet Jeremiah likens us to, "

> *He is like a tree planted by water, that sends out its roots by the stream, and does not fear when heat comes, for its leaves remain green, and is not anxious in the year of drought, for it does not cease to bear fruit.*
> *(Jeremiah 17:8)*

Indeed, we are the tree that the prophet speaks of in the above passage. The LORD requires that there be no cessation in *bearing fruit,* even when we experience the heat/trouble or lack—*in the year of drought.* I can testify that during my 'stormy season' I found much peace, joy, energy, and strength to bear even more *fruit* for the LORD.

Jesus continues to deliver a powerful, perpetual message on *bearing fruit* as if to drill this message inside of His disciples. He re-emphasizes, *"You did not choose me, but I chose you and appointed you that you should go and bear fruit, and that your fruit should abide, that whatever you ask the Father in my name He may give to you. These things I command you, that you love one another" (John 15:16-17).* I believe if we, the believers, would allow that particular passage of Scripture to resonate in our spirits, we would witness a changed world for Christ. We would be witnessing to the lost like we have never seen or done before. Moreover, every opportunity that is given us, not only will we seek the LORD for our individual assignments, but discover what they are and do them. We speak of glorifying God interminably in our church services Sunday after Sunday, but we limit it to praise and worship. However, the preceding Scriptures are evidence that God desires to be glorified in our *Works* too, which means to *bear fruit*. It is worth mentioning that the LORD is so adamant about our *bearing fruit* in everything that He requires it even when we repent. When the Pharisees and Sadducees' came to the Jordan River to be baptized by John the Baptist, John quickly reprimanded them and assigned them the appellation, 'snakes'. He says this, *"You brood of vipers, who warned you to flee from the wrath to come? You need to bear fruit that befits repentance" (Matthew 3:7-8).* Clearly, John is saying that the proof of a penitent heart is not just words, but rather it is the *bearing of fruit* that shows we are serious and sorry for our sins and to do the *Works* that are congruous to repentance. For one, we can win souls for the LORD. After all, Scripture teaches us this very fact, *"Let him know that whoever brings back a sinner from his wandering will save his soul from death and will cover a multitude of sins" (James 5:20).* Apostle Paul released a powerful testimony before King Agrippa with regards to the main purpose of his 'calling' and mentions repentance in his discourse. As he gave a testimony of his initial meeting with the LORD, he says this,

THE POWER OF KNOW

> *Wherefore, O King Agrippa, I was not disobedient to the heavenly vision, but declared first to those at Damascus, then at Jerusalem and throughout all the country of Judea, and also to the Gentiles, that they should repent and turn to God and perform deeds worthy of their repentance.*
>
> *Acts 26:19-20)*

Paul's testimony before King Agrippa echoes the words that Jesus spoke—that we should *bear fruit* that befits repentance by doing the *Works*— *perform deeds worthy of their repentance.* If we are constantly before the throne of God daily asking for forgiveness, the LORD wants us to produce some *fruit* that shows that we are Godly sorry for our trespasses; and we don't expect to do them again. In other words, our *Works* should reflect our repentance. One thing that is interesting about one of the aforementioned passages is that our Father is not interested in our JUST *bearing fruit,* but that our *fruit abides.* Plainly stated, the *fruit* which we produce should stay, remain, be impactful. For the *fruit* to *abide*, it must have an interminable effect. Plainly speaking, the *fruit* we bear should not spoil nor rotten. Even when we have stopped or rested, the *fruit* is always at *Work.* There is a time, however, that we pause, not stop, for a sabbath rest, or for a time of meditation and reflection. What we do for the Kingdom of God should *abide* or remain so that the LORD is constantly being glorified. Perhaps the poet C.T. Studd had this revelation when he pens, "Only one life, 'twill soon be past,' only what's done for Christ will last." The *Works* we do remain or last because it is the LORD working through us. What we have put our hands and heart to do for the Kingdom of God should have a lasting impact even when we leave the Earth. In other words, we should leave a 'legacy' of *abiding fruit*. Whatever good *Works* we *perform* in our family, church, community, and society should be so impactful that it will be a blessing to later generations and cause the LORD's name to be always celebrated. Any ministry, i.e., causes, soul winning, witnessing, preaching, testimonies, teachings, offerings, books we have written that cause people to be saved, drawn closer to God are considered *abiding fruit*. Any individual God-given assignments that CHANGE the lives of others and leave a lasting imprint, are considered *abiding fruit*. Our *Works, bearing fruit,* and more importantly, *abiding fruit,* is what glorifies God! Jesus encourages us in Scripture by saying, *"Let your light so shine before men that they may see your good works and give glory to your Father, who is heaven"* (Matthew 5:16).

CHAPTER 20
STAR *Power* or *Star Struck?*

We must be cognizant of the fact that as we produce *abiding fruit,* we are *Performing* the *Great Exploits* in the Earth to which we have been called. Equally important is the fact that our relationship, kinship, and friendship with God play a significant role in the *Great Exploits* that the LORD promises to do in and through us. As noted in the previous chapter, without a fellowship with the Great King, our physical labor/*Works* are nominal. "But what are some of the other *Works* that the LORD requires of us?" For one, the believer has been called to *Witness* to the masses. Being in His manifest Presence, I have discovered that Evangelism is an important component of God's *Great Exploits* and very close to the LORD's heart. Without question, one of the greatest *Works* we can do for the Master is to win souls. I have testified of the importance of winning souls for the LORD in various platforms that the LORD has given me to stand and minister along with the numerous books that I have written. I reiterate that message so profoundly because the LORD has spoken those words to my *KNOW*. I am totally convinced that this is the main *Work* of the church, individually and collectively. The LORD is very passionate about saving the lost. Because He is passionate about the lost, it has also become my passion. As a matter of fact, before a year comes to its end, I committed myself to winning at least one soul for the Kingdom. I am determined to win more but committed to win at least one. For the Word declares in 2 Peter these words, *"The LORD is not slow to fulfill his promise as some count slowness, but is patient toward you, not wishing that any should perish, but that all should reach repentance" (3:9).* The preceding Scripture speaks the heart of God succinctly, declaring that the LORD desires that none would perish and go to hell—that all would be saved. Unfortunately, it will not be the case; and He knows that too. However, it does not give us, the believers, a pretext for not doing the *Work*. Consequently, He has equipped the saints with the necessary resources to do this great *Work*. And He is seeking *STARS* to do it. "What are *STARS*?" *STARS* are God's people who are adamant about leading the 'lost' to Him. They are also <u>those</u> whom Daniels speaks of in this passage, *"And those who are wise shall shine like the brightness of the sky above; and those who turn many to righteousness, like the stars forever and ever" (Daniel 12:3).* *STAR-Powered* believers are those who do the *Work* of the Evangelist as Apostle Paul so eloquently encourages us to do, *"As for you, always be sober-minded, endure suffering, do the work of an evangelist, fulfill your ministry" (2 Timothy 4:5).* According to this passage, any ministry we do for the Master is incomplete if we do not do the work of an Evangelist. I am afraid that in the age of technology, there are many believers who have become *Star-Struck* and consumed with the so-called stars or celebrities in the entertainment, sports, news media, social media, and business world. Let me say parenthetically that technology is a great tool to use to advance the Kingdom of God. From observation, however, I have seen how Facebook, Twitter, Instagram, You Tube, and other social media platforms are being used by the people of God to influence people for the purpose of developing a 'following' or STARdom status or popularity for themselves. Much of that 'following' leads people to THEM in lieu of the King. These mediums are popular and have become people's major support mechanisms, and they give some of them a false sense of worth, security, and identity. Consequently, they find 'rest' in knowing that they have hundreds, thousands, or even millions of people who 'follow' and 'LIKE' them on these platforms. For some believers, these media outlets have replaced the safety and security that God provides for them for the security of others. If we, the believers, use these social media platforms to gain popularity or celebrity/STARdom status ONLY and do not lead people to God, they may lead to PRIDE. They fail to realize that God has called them to stand, take their place, and be counted as the real *STARS* and be *STAR-Powered* according to His definition. Of course, that entails doing the *Works*, witnessing to the 'lost' and winning them over to His Kingdom. While we perform such duties for the King, we receive a blessing as stated in the book of James, *"Let him know that whoever brings back a sinner from his wandering will save his soul from death and will cover a multitude of sins" (5:20).* According to James, when we cause someone to turn from their sinful nature to God, it keeps our souls even from death and cover a plethora of sins we have committed. Winning the 'lost' to the LORD also testify to our wisdom. This is what Solomon pens in the book of Proverbs, *"The fruit of the righteous is a tree of life, and he who is wise wins souls" (11:30).* Surely, there is *Power* in our *Witness/Works*. And they who KNOW the LORD do *Great Exploits* by bringing the 'unsaved' to Him. They are not Star-Struck but rather *STAR-Powered!*

CHAPTER 21
The *Fear* of the LORD
A *Strategy* to *Persuade*

Because the *Witness/Works* of the LORD are very precious to HIM, and it is the greatest *Work* of the church, He has given us the tools and the *strategy* to *perform* them. For one, having a *Knowledge* of the *Fear of the LORD* can cause us to be impactful in our *Witness*. I reiterate the fact that the LORD's earnest desire is for us to win the lost to Him. And yes, the LORD gives us individual assignments to do in His Kingdom too. However, above all, we are required to *Witness* to the lost. For He has clearly revealed to me personally that *Evangelism* is His passion. He also spoke these words very clearly to me, "You Have Been Chosen To Be A Witness". In the world in which we live today, the devil is doing his work in our families, communities, cities, nation, and literally across the world. That includes in the home, workplace, school, church, government, etc. Moreover, we reside in a multi-cultural/diversified society today; and people of various religious facets, cults, etc. are recruiting and competing with one another for the purpose of influences many to crossover and be a part of their so-called doctrines, beliefs, ideologies, etc. With the various religious groups working against the church of Jesus Christ today, it can be very cumbersome not only to witness to the lost but win them to the LORD. I have been in the streets for many years evangelizing for the LORD. Many years ago, it was much easier to win the lost than today. There is, indeed, a stronghold of the devil on many, especially the young men and women. However, I have also discovered that it will take a *strategy,* secret weapon in our arsenal that many rarely think possible to use. One of the weapons is the *testimony of God* (I John 5:9). I elaborated on *the testimony of God* in the books, *"A Report From The Heights"* and *"You're Welcome, The Power of Giving Thanks"*. Just as lethal and powerful as the *testimony of God* is, there is another that we may not be acquainted with nor used often; and that is the F*ear of the LORD.* When the Apostle Paul and the others witnessed for Jesus in various parts of the world, they tapped into this powerful *strategy/tool*; and they operated in it. It came by way of their *Knowledge* of the *Fear of God.* This is what Paul speaks to the church at Corinth, *"Knowing therefore the fear of the LORD, we persuade men..." (2 Corinthians 5:11).* Apostle Paul and his apostolic team realized that they needed something more powerful than just saying a few words or verses to capture the people's attention to win them over to the LORD. Because they needed *The Fear of the LORD*, they had a revelation of it; and it became *Power* for them in the *Works.* "What is the *Fear of the LORD*, and why is it so impactful in *persuading* people?" When we reverence and respect the LORD, we give the LORD His due—that which we owe Him. If we desire to tap into the treasure/heart of God, we must have a reverence and respect for Him. No doubt, the *Fear of the LORD* is significant in the believer's walk with God. More than anytime, it is desperately needed in the body of Christ. According to Solomon, the writer of Proverbs, it is the prelude to *Knowledge* (Proverbs 1:7). Plainly stated, we cannot obtain the *Knowledge* of God unless we **FIRST** fear Him. David had come to the revelation that one cannot *KNOW the Fear of the LORD* unless the LORD teaches it. Apparently, the LORD taught him so that he might instruct generations later. He says these words in Psalms,

> *Come O sons, listen to me, and I will teach you the fear of the LORD. What man is there who desires life and covets many days, that he may enjoy good? Let him keep his mouth from evil and his lips from speaking deceits. Let him depart from evil and do good. Let him seek peace and pursue it. The eyes of the LORD are toward the righteous and his ear toward their cries, but his face is against evildoers.*
>
> *(34:11-15)*

I believe it was David's teaching and words of wisdom that the apostles possessed which enabled them to be as impactful as they were in their ministry of *persuading* the people. As a matter of fact, David himself applied that same wisdom in an unusual situation he was faced with. As he encountered his enemy, Saul, who had constantly pursued him, relieving himself in a cave, he did not kill him. Even when the men whom he traveled with urged him to kill Saul, he was inexorable. These are the words of his passe, "Here is the day of which the LORD said to you, 'Behold, I will give your enemy into your hand, and you shall do to him as it shall seem good to you'" (I Samuel 24:4). Surely, the men's words echo, "David, You Got Him! The LORD Has Finally Delivered The Enemy Into Your Hands! Now Do As You

THE POWER OF KNOW

Please!" However, David had such a reverence for God that his conscience would not allow him to perform what the men apparently expected him to do—kill Saul! This is David's response to the men, *"The LORD forbid that I should do this thing to my lord, the LORD's anointed, to put forth my hand against him, seeing he is the LORD's anointed" (I Samuel 24:6)*. One would rarely find a man on Earth who would have allowed this man to escape from him. Many believers would have found themselves rejoicing in this 'great spoil'. However, the *'spirit of the Fear of the LORD'* was upon David. Not only did he refrain from touching Saul because of his respect for God and His anointed, but he was able to *persuade* the men to follow his lead. *"So David persuaded his men with these words, and did not permit them to attack Saul" (I Samuel 24:7)*. The men apparently saw David's genuine respect for the LORD; and they obeyed him, even when they felt Saul was 'worthy' of death.

Abraham also had a revelation of the *Fear of the LORD* to the degree that he was able to discern the absence of it in Egypt. Of course, some would call what he did a lie when he told the nation's king that Sarah was his sister instead of his wife. Later, when the king admonished him for his words, this was Abraham's alibi, *"I did it because I thought, 'There is no fear of God at all in this place, and they will kill me because of my wife'" (Genesis 20:11)*. This man had a revelation that when there is no *Fear of God* among people in a place, violence, death, and destruction are imminent. Let me parenthetically say that, I don't believe what Abraham did was considered a lie in the sight of God but rather he exercised sound wisdom that preserved him and his wife from death. Like Abraham, the

The *Fear* of the LORD—*A Strategy* to *Persuade*

Hebrew midwives who preserved the male babies in Egypt from being destroyed at the decree of Pharaoh, operated in the *Fear of God.* When the king of Egypt commanded them to carry out such a cruel act against their people and, of course, God's children, they disobeyed him. When the king of Egypt reprimanded them, they did not lie but exercised sound wisdom. They stated that they were unable to stop the rapid births because the Israelite women were too strong and vigorous and before they arrived to deliver the babies, the women had already given birth. In reality, the reason they saved the male children was because they *feared* God. Scripture says, *"But the midwives feared God and did not do as the king of Egypt commanded them, but let the male children live" (Exodus 1:17).* Their *Knowledge* of the *Fear of God* was ingrained in them to the degree that they were able to convince/*persuade* the king of Egypt that they were telling the truth. Today's society is replete with violence, destruction; and evil is rife. Consequently, the LORD seeks people that will walk in the *Fear of the LORD* like never before, not just to LIVE but for the purpose of advancing the Kingdom of God.

Needless to say, in order to bring change in a crooked, corrupt, mean and evil society, we need the *Fear of the LORD.* When Paul and the rest of the apostles had *Knowledge* of the *Fear of the LORD,* they spoke of the Resurrection of Jesus; and they were totally committed, convinced, 'souled/sold out' to the LORD. They had experienced this Christ in a Supernatural unusual way and had daily encounters with Him. Accordingly, when they spoke of the LORD to those whom they were witnessing, the hearers were able to discern whether they were 'phonies' or not. People saw that they had a genuine reverence and respect for Christ, and they knew that their testimony was real because the Spirit of the LORD rested upon them. Not only did they have the Spirit of wisdom, understanding, knowledge, counsel and might, but the *Spirit of the Fear of the LORD (Isaiah 11:2)*. <u>KNOWING</u> *The Fear of the LORD*, they taught with authority as Jesus did, and they were effective in speaking the Truth and *persuading* others to receive the Christ as their Savior and LORD. No doubt, <u>KNOWING</u> *the Fear of the LORD* is a powerful Evangelistic *strategy* for convincing others to take the LORD's side. The prophet Jonah applied it wisely while he was on the ship headed for Tarshish. When the men on the ship, who traveled with Jonah experienced a raucous journey, they attempted to throw him overboard because they perceived him to be the culprit or omen. Apparently, they did not *KNOW* God. They believed Jonah was the reason for the turmoil they were experiencing, and they interrogated him. This is what they said, *"Tell us, on whose account this evil has come upon us? What is your occupation? And whence do you come? What is your country? And of what people are you?" (Jonah 1:8).* This is how Jonah responded to the men, *"I am a Hebrew and I fear the LORD, the God of heaven, who made the sea and the dry land" (Jonah 1:8-9).* Surely, we can glean some wisdom from his simple response. When we are witnessing to people on the streets and other places, so often we tell them what we think they should hear instead of what they <u>need</u> to hear. No doubt, our personal testimonies of what God has done for us matters. However, Jonah did not go through a long drawn out speech or conversation about who he was. He simply told them his nationality, that he *feared* the LORD; and he gave a laconic explanation of who God is, *the God of heaven, who made the sea and the dry land.* In other words, what the men heard from Jonah was about <u>HIM</u>, the LORD, and not about <u>him</u>. However, the key clause that convinced/*persuaded* these men was, "*I Fear The LORD.*" Indeed, there is *Power* in KNOWING the *Fear of the LORD.* When we possess that *Knowledge*, we walk in accordance with it. We *KNOW* that Jesus/The Holy Spirit lives in us, that He is sitting directly in our presence every minute, second, hour, and that it is required of us to conduct ourselves accordingly. I believe that this is the type of reverence and respect for the Master He wants from His children. Being in the Presence of the LORD daily, I strive to attain to that level of respect for Him.

Like Paul and the apostles, the LORD wants us to convince, *persuade* and 'snatch back' those who are under the stronghold of the enemy and who are headed for destruction. Paul and the other apostles used a God-proof *STRATEGY*, an approved method, that cannot be compared to any other. They used the *Fear of God* to influence or *persuade* men. Like Jesus, any 'followers' they picked up led them to Elohim/ HIM and NOT <u>them</u>. *KNOWING the Fear of the LORD,* gives us assurance, confidence, and enables us to be effective and impactful in ministry and to accomplish the mission of *persuading* to advance the Kingdom of the LORD.

CHAPTER 22
Rewards
What's Your *Credit Score?*

We have already discussed in previous chapters that our *Works* have much to do with the love we express in our relationship to God, i.e., spending time with the LORD, seeking His Face daily, extolling His *Works* and, of course, *Performing His Works.* From time to time, we hear words via sermons, teachings, etc. that 'serving God pays off.' Rightly so, it does. We, however, do not *perform* His deeds for the mere purpose of getting paid. We do it because He is God, He deserves it, and He commands us to do it! After all, "What shall we render to God for all of His benefits?" However, God is such a faithful, loving God that He will *Reward* us for the *Works* we *perform.* In the book of Jeremiah, He encourages His People who were in a foreign land because of their disobedience, with these words, *"Restrain your voice from weeping and your eyes from tears, for your work will be rewarded,"* declares the LORD (31:16). In another passage of Scripture, the LORD says the same to King Asa, *"But you, take courage! Do not let your hands be weak, for your work shall be rewarded"* (2 Chronicles 15:7). Occasionally, in the assignments the LORD gives, we might become fatigued, tired, and weary. However, He reminds us not to be weary in well doing, for we shall reap if we do not faint (Galatians 6:9). The above passages are indicative of the fact that God does not forget the *Works* we *perform* to advance His Kingdom. And He is forever encouraging as we do His *Works*. I remember being so exhausted from a few assignments God had given me to do, hearing Him very clearly say, "Your Labor Is Not In Vain". When He spoke those words, I was at an ATM Drive-Thru line at a bank, and I found so much joy in hearing the LORD encourage me. From those words, I gained new spiritual and physical energy to continue in the *Work* because I KNEW that He had not forgotten me. The LORD reminds His People that man will forget any kindness we render to them, but He will not forget us. Anyway, they cannot *Reward* us in the manner in which the LORD does. In the book of Isaiah, He reminds His people of His faithfulness by saying, *"Can a woman forget her nursing child, that she should have no compassion on the son of her womb? Even these may forget, yet I will not forget you" (49:15).* It is good to KNOW that God will always remember us. Likewise, Jesus reminds us to always be faithful. He also reminds us of the *Rewards* that proceed our loyalty and faithfulness towards Him. He says, *"If you remain in me and my words remain in you, ask whatever you wish, and it will be done for you. Herein is my Father glorified, that ye bear much fruit; so shall prove to be my disciples" (John 15:7-11).* Aforementioned in the previous chapter, God wants to be glorified in everything; and when we CONTINUE in the *Works*, He assures us that we will not only be *Rewarded* by granting our requests, but prove to be His disciples. I would be remised if I failed to mention the fact that the LORD has already promised that He *Rewards* those who will go after Him, *"For whoever would draw near to God must believe that he exists and that he rewards*

Rewards—What's Your Credit Score?

those who diligently seek him" (Hebrews 11:6). When we seek the LORD and find Him, we are guaranteed a *Reward*. What a loving and faithful God we serve who will *Reward* us for diligently 'looking' for Him!

<u>Good Credit!</u>

It is worth noting that God has another way of showing favor to His People. Just as we strive to acquire a favorable credit score or qualify to obtain some things we dream that we would have in life, i.e., beautiful homes, cars, apparel, real estate, business, a mate, family, etc., I believe the LORD has a system He uses to *Reward* loyal saints who touch His heart in a very significant way. It is by way of *credits*. These *credits* go beyond our Christian duty, for our Christian duty is to do what is expected of us (Luke 17:10). The manner in which we touch God's heart plays a significant role in obtaining this *credit*. First, our faith coupled with our *Works* allows us to receive a score. James reminds us that *"faith without works is dead" (2:14-26).* However, coming into full *Knowledge* of the **ONE** thing that touches God's heart will allow us to obtain a score which overflows into a myriad of blessings. As Jesus walked and taught in the Earth, He often spoke of obtaining *credits.* For instance, He spoke these words, *"If you love those who love you, what credit is that to you? For even sinners love those who love them. And if you do good to those who do good to you, what credit is that to you? For even sinners do the same" (Luke 6:32-33).* Clearly, these passages allow us to see that the LORD is interested in *Rewarding* us with *credits* for the *Works* we *perform* outside of what is required of us. Furthermore, Peter echoes Jesus' words as he speaks of how to obtain *credits* from the LORD when he says this, *"For what credit is it, when you sin and are beaten for it, you endure? But if when you do good and suffer for it you endure, this is a gracious thing in the sight of God"* (I Peter 2:20). Peter allows us to see that when we do wrong and get punished for it and survive the punishment, we should not receive any recognition. The 'beat down' was a consequence for doing wrong. Plainly stated, those actions result in obtaining 'zero credit'. However, if we do right and receive punishment for it, that is something that God recognizes; and it is *credited* to us. In other words, we receive no *credit* unless we endure through suffering when we do good. It is important to note that acquiring these *credits* are not synonymous to receiving 'brownie points'. As a matter of fact, they are the complete antithesis. 'Brownie Points' usually stem from deception, sell-outs, selfishness, jealousy, and envy. Moreover, they derive from individuals who attempt to present themselves as 'good' in the face of someone in authority with the intent of gaining an advantage over another. Usually, those who desire 'brownie points' desire to be promoted in various positions of authority, business, i.e., the workplace, even the church. Again, they are usually opportunists who try to elevate themselves in the presence of someone in authority. I liken one who desires 'brownie points' to Pharaoh's chief butler who was in prison with Joseph. While they were incarcerated, Joseph, who was falsely accused, interpreted his dream, which pleased him. Later, the chief butler was acquitted of his crime. Prior to his release, Joseph asked the chief butler if

Rewards—What's Your *Credit Score?*

he would remember him and speak kind words on his behalf to Pharaoh with the intent that he too would be exonerated. *"But think of me when it shall be well with thee, and shew kindness, I pray thee, unto me, and make mention of me unto Pharaoh, and bring me out of this house" (Genesis 40:14).* Upon his release, this is what happened next, *"Yet the chief butler did not remember Joseph, but forgot him" (Genesis 40:23).* Ironically, two years later the chief butler remembered the words Joseph had requested that he relay to Pharaoh. It was the time when he could acquire 'brownie points'. Pharaoh had a dream and sought and interpreter, and none was found throughout Egypt. Suddenly, the chief butler remembered what Joseph did for him and Pharaoh's baker, who had also been incarcerated with them. Now, he speaks these words to Pharaoh,

> *And there was there with us a young man, a Hebrew, servant to the captain of the guard; and we told him, and he interpreted to us our dreams; to each man according to his dream he did interpret.*
>
> *(Genesis 41:12).*

The chief butler found an opportunity THEN to present himself in the eyes of Pharaoh in naming the one person who could do this great thing for Pharaoh. Even though the Bible does not state what gifts, favor, or even promotion was bestowed upon him, if any, the 'points' came at the suffering of Joseph being left in a jail for two additional years for a crime he did not commit. However, it still worked in Joseph's favor because not only was he released, he received a promotion, which was second in command to Pharaoh.

THE POWER OF KNOW

In the Bible, there were a few who received *credit* for the manner in which they touched the very heart of God. Abraham received the utmost *credit* for his *Works* in the form of Belief/Faith in just the words which God spoke when He made a promise to him. Because he believed God, he received *credit*. *"And he believed in the LORD, and it was credited to him as righteousness" (Genesis 15:5-6)*. Because our FIRST *Works* is to believe, Abraham received the promise and became the father of all because his *Works* in the form of *faith* caused him to be blessed immensely. No doubt, his faith in the Promise enabled him to obtain the highest *credit* score of all. Next, Phinehas the priest, Aaron's grandson, received an excellent *credit score* when he averted a plague that God sent which killed thousands of the children of Israel. These words were penned in the book of Psalms for the actions of Phinehas, *"Then Phinehas stood up and interposed and the plague was stayed. And that has been reckoned (credited) to him as righteousness from generation to generation forever" (Psalms 106:31)*. In response to what Phinehas did, this is what the LORD says as He *credits* him,

> *And the LORD said to Moses, Phinehas the son of Eleazar son of Aaron the priest, has turned back my wrath from the people of Israel in that he was jealous with my jealousy among them, so that I did not consume the people of Israel in my jealousy. Therefore, say, 'Behold, I give to him my covenant of peace; and it shall be to him, and to his descendants after him, the covenant of a perpetual priesthood, because he was jealous for his God, and made atonement for the people of Israel.'*
>
> *(Numbers 25:10-13)*

Rewards—What's Your *Credit Score?*

Surely, this man's jealousy for the heart of God moved him to take a stand for God; and he was blessed tremendously. As a result of his *Works*, he received a *covenant* of peace and priesthood forever, which was attributed to him as righteousness in the form of *credit*. Needless to say, Caleb and Joshua received *credit* when Moses sent them to spy out the land. Unlike the other leaders who accompanied them, they did not return with a nefarious report that frighten the people. They 'wholly' followed the LORD, and they touched God's heart in a very special way. From the 12 leaders who were sent, they were the only ones who were blessed to enter the Promise Land and be recipients of their inheritance (Numbers 32:10-12). Aforementioned in the previous chapter, David did something that no one would have ever done in his refusal to kill Saul when God delivered Saul into his hands. And God *Rewarded* him. The LORD even allowed Saul who had constantly chased him to speak the blessing upon him. This is what Saul says to David,

> *For if a man finds his enemy, will he let him go away safe? So may the LORD reward you with good for what you have done to me this day. And now I know that you shall surely be king, and that the kingdom of Israel shall be established in your hand.*
> *(I Samuel 24:17-20)*

No doubt, King David was greatly *credited* for the manner in which he handled the situation involving Saul. More importantly, God remembered him. Apostle Paul had a revelation of the blessings in the form of *credits* that we, the believers, could receive from God to the degree that he reminded the people of God who bestowed upon him their gifts. This is what he says,

> *And you Philippians yourselves know that in the beginning of the gospel, when I left Macedonia, no church entered into partnership with me in giving and receiving except you only; for even in Thessalonica you sent me help once and again. Not that I seek the gift; but I seek the fruit which increases to your credit... a fragrant offering, a sacrifice acceptable and pleasing to God.*
> *(Philippians 4:15-18)*

At the ministry's inception and among the many churches Paul had visited, none gave to Paul except the church in Philippi. He expressed his gratitude to them for their exceptional kindness by letting them know that in giving to him, they were rendering to God their *fruit/offering*. Because the church in Philippi did something unusual by blessing Paul with a gift that NO other church had done and because it was freely given from the heart, it became *credit* for them. It became a fragrant, sweet smelling sacrificial offering, which is always pleasing to the LORD. Outside of the gift Paul had received from them, more than anything, he was interested in the church increasing their *credit score*, thereby becoming the benefactors of the blessings of God. He reminded the people the way in which God would bless them for their tremendous generosity, *"And my God shall supply every need of yours according to his riches in glory in Christ Jesus"* (Philippians 4:19). In essence, when we give from the heart, we touch the heart of God in a special way. That Scripture becomes applicable not just to the church at Philippi but to all who *perform* such *Works*. It is surely worth mentioning Ruth, who was tremendously *credited* for the manner in which she exemplified kindness to her mother-in-law, Naomi. This is what her future husband Boaz tells her,

> *All that you have done for your mother-in-law since the death of your husband has been fully told me, and how you left your father and mother and your native land and came to a people that you did not know before.*
> *(Ruth 2:11)*

For the <u>ONE</u> thing Ruth did for her mother-in-law that apparently touched the LORD's heart, Boaz pronounced the blessing upon her, *"The LORD recompense you for what you have done, and a full reward be given you by the LORD, the God of Israel, under whose wings you have come to take refuge!" (Ruth 2:12)*. Indeed, Ruth, having to endure grief herself from the loss of her husband, sacrificed much. Seeing nothing to be gained, she left her family to travel to a land she was unfamiliar with. However, she knew the pain and heartache her mother-in-law Naomi had endured, having lost her husband and two sons. But she refused to leave her in her plight. Instead, she chose to remain with her. God saw her heart and greatly *credited* her by giving her a wealthy husband and children. Out of her lineage was a great grandson named King David and, of course, Jesus Christ our Savior and LORD who also proceeded from that lineage.

Moreover, in the book of Esther, there is mention of a man named Mordecai, Esther's cousin, who was greatly *Rewarded* by King Ahasuerus, reigning king of Persia. Mordecai received a promotion because he prevented two 'backstabbing' servants of the king from killing King Ahasuerus. Mordecai heard the plot, and he revealed it to Esther who told the king. Any great deeds done for the kingdom was written in a book of Memorable Deeds, and Mordecai's name had been written in the book. However, it appeared that Mordecai had been forgotten; and he had never received *credit* for his deed in saving the life of the king by unfolding this vicious plot. This is what happened though,

> *On that night the king could not sleep; and he gave orders to bring the book of memorable deeds, the chronicles, and they were read before the king. And it was found written how Mordecai had told about Bigthana and Teresh, two of the king's eunuchs, who guarded the threshold, and who sought to lay hands upon King Ahasuerus.*
> *(Esther 6:1-2)*

I believe God, whose name is not mentioned in the book of Esther, but deemed very present, caused King Ahasuerus to have a restless night in order to bring the deeds of Mordecai to his remembrance. After the king recalls the *Works* of Mordecai, this is what he says next, "What honor or dignity has been bestowed on Mordecai for this?" (Esther 6:3) Needless to say, King Ahasuerus showed extraordinary kindness to Mordecai; and he was promoted in a great way. If an idolatrous king would possess a book of 'Memorable Deeds',

Rewards—What's Your *Credit Score?*

surely the Great King of kings has a book of 'Memorial Deeds' that He uses to record our names for the deeds we *perform* in the Earth that are 'heart-felt'. God will always remember our *Works* as the king remembered Mordecai's; and like his, ours will be recorded in His 'book of Memorable Deeds.' As previously noted, Jesus has already done the complete *Work* when He died on the Cross. Truly, it is by His *Works* that God sees our *Works*! Therefore, it is He who *credits* us.

Indeed, the LORD *credits* us with special favors for the **ONE** thing we do for Him and others that greatly please Him. God's ultimate desire is to bless His people; and when we touch His heart in a special way while we journey with Him, it will be *credited* to us. It becomes a pleasing odor to the LORD, enabling us to receive manifold, unusual, unexpected blessings. In return, we, too, will receive an excellent *credit score* as He greatly *Rewards* us! "What *Works* will or do <u>you</u> *perform* by FAITH from the heart that reaches the very heart of God ABOVE that which is expected of you to your *credit?*"

> "For the LORD rewards every man for his righteousness and his faithfulness."
>
> (I Samuel 26:23)

> "And, behold, I come quickly; and my reward is with me, to give every man according as his work shall be."
>
> (Revelations 22:12)

Summary

We have concluded that *KNOW* has *Power* if we allow it; and God, our Heavenly Father, wants His people to *KNOW* it! *The Power of KNOW* in the *Word* can transform our lives totally for the LORD when we become knowledgeable of the Truth and we walk in it. *The Power of KNOW* in our *Worship* can become a weapon that sets the atmosphere in our homes, cities, neighborhoods, workplace, church, and causes us to constantly see and experience the LORD's Salvation, His Glory, His FIRE. More than anything, it will give the LORD His due. Certainly, the *Power of KNOW* in our *Works* can transform our society/culture, which includes our schools, neighborhood, cities, nation, and even the various systems of this world, thereby leading many to the LORD. That *Knowledge* includes having a full understanding and coming into total agreement with God that we have a *Purpose* and calling in the Earth, which allows us to LIVE a fruitful and productive life! As I complete the writing of this book, the world is in a turmoil with an uncontrollable pandemic COVID-19 virus that is infecting and killing millions of people. The workplace, churches, businesses, schools, etc. have literally been shut down. The economy is dubious, and it appears that recovery is not imminent for some time soon. However, God reminds me that He is in control! I strongly believe that God wants to discipline us, and He desires for us to come into such a *Knowledge*, understanding, and revelation of who He is that He is willing to do us a favor by shutting down everything to allow people time to just BE STILL and *KNOW* Him! The LORD reminds us in His Word to, *"Be still, and know that I am God. I am exalted among the nations, I am exalted in the earth!" (Psalms 46:10).* With certainty, when we are still and listen to the Voice of God, we will *KNOW* BETTER; and when we *KNOW* BETTER, the LORD expects us to <u>*DO*</u> BETTER. For the LORD says,

Keep the **Faith**
Keep **Believing**
and
KNOW
He is the LORD God!

Notes

Notes

Other Sonflower Publishing Titles

Revelation Reading
to help you grow spiritually in reading

Inheriting His Holy Mountain
by Herstine Wright

ISBN: 0-9713416-0-5
Category: Christian Education;
Devotional: Praise/Worship
Price: $14.99

A personal testimony and powerful teaching with scriptural references of:

- Getting <u>to</u> God's manifest Presence
- Getting <u>into</u> God's manifest Presence
- <u>Remaining in</u> God's manifest Presence
- <u>Obtaining the blessing of</u> being in God's manifest Presence

"As a 'worshipper' I must declare that Herstine Wright has powerfully opened a door in the Spirit for those who truly want to experience the Kingdom through pursuing His presence. It is principled. It is purposeful. It is practical! Inheriting His Holy Mountain is a must read for new believers and seasoned saints alike desiring the greatest inheritance of all, Christ!"

–Apostle Daryl O'Neil
Senior Pastor
Ruach Covenant Church Int'l

Discovering God's Sacred SECRETS
by Herstine Wright

ISBN: 978-0-9713416-9-2
Category: Christian Education;
Devotional: Praise/Worship
Price: $19.99

Discovering God's Sacred SECRETS is a valuable teaching tool that aids the believer in unfolding God's most treasured blessing by revealing who God gives His *Secrets* to; the place to find His *Secrets;* and the Divine purpose for revealing His *Secrets.* By tapping into the mysteries of God, we see our purpose for living in the *Kingdom* of God.

Order Your Copy Today!

Ask for it at your local Christian bookstore or order it online.

"A flower of the Son blossoms into a wonder"

For more information visit our website at
www.sonflowerpublishing.com

Other Sonflower Publishing Titles

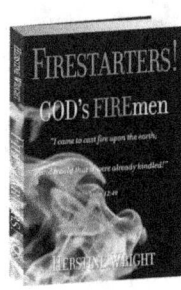

**FIRESTARTERS!
GOD's FIREmen
by Herstine Wright**

ISBN: 978-0-9713416-4-7
Category: Christian Education;
Devotional: Praise/Worship
Price: $19.99

FIRESTARTERS! GOD's Firemen is a book of Worship and Authority. It is also a revelation of the baptism of FIRE and the purpose of God's Presence that resides in us.

I ordered this book from a conference I went to hoping I could understand God's presence and what does it mean to have fire. This book brought understanding and desire! The author has given all kinds of illustrations of God's fire in the book and she references scriptures (which is the best proof there is). I have to admit I was brought to repentance for how selfish I have treated God and repented when I got to the section about worship. I really recommend this book for Christians to read because we need God's presence in our schools, homes, and everywhere we go. This book along w/the Holy Spirit will take you deeper to the Father!

–mSmilez
Amazon.com review

**Jesus and
The New Math
2 + 5=5000
by Regenia S. Wright**

ISBN: 978-09713416-8-5
Category: Christian Education; Children
Price: $12.99

"Jesus and The New Math 2 + 5=5,000" is written for children of all ages. It is a depiction of the compassion and miraculous power of our LORD and Savior. In accordance with the theme, it also reminds readers today of the great things that happen as a result of following Jesus.

Order Your Copy Today!

Ask for it at your

local Christian

bookstore

or order it online.

*"A flower of
the Son blossoms
into a wonder"*

**For more
information visit
our website at
www.sonflowerpublishing.com**

Other Sonflower Publishing Titles

The Essence of A Lady
by Reneé L. Gilkey

ISBN: 0-9713416-2-5
Category: Christian Education;
Devotional: Women
Price: $14.99

If you think this book is about being prim and proper, it is not. If the name suggests a picture perfect female in stiletto heels and a silky chiffon dress, that is not the message. *The Essence of a Lady* is simply a tool to help you discover and accept your awesomeness. It will open your eyes to the magnum opus (masterpiece) God created when He made YOU!

"With candor and commitment, she often goes against the grain of contemporary society, debunking the philosophy of the so-called women's liberation movement while calling for a re-establishment of such values as femininity, etiquette, physical beauty that does not bow down to Madison Avenue's definition."

–Bishop Kenneth C. Ulmer,
D. Min., Ph.D.
Faithful Central Bible Church

Why Would A Child Lie?
by Rose Williams

ISBN: 0-9713416-3-x
Category: Christian Education;
Devotional: Women
Price: $15.99

Journey with the author, Rose Williams, as she unfolds eight critical years of her life having endured incestual abuse. She maps out her road to recovery and forgiveness and lists ways of identifying and exposing these types of relationships.

Many Are Called But Few Are Chosen
by Randall Morgan

ISBN: 0-9713416-1-3
Category: Christian Education/Devotional
Price: $12.95

Everyone is born on purpose with a purpose. There are no accidents. God took advantage of an opportunity to get you into the earth to do His Will, no matter what that opportunity was. The mystery of your personal assignment is that it is not printed on your birth certificate, only your birth is.

Many Are Called But Few Are Chosen is an eight chapter book that is vibrant and dynamic. It is alive, and it lives to transform "the called" into "the chosen".

"I loved reading this book. It was very inspirational, and I will take it with me wherever I go."

–Lloyd McClendon
Former Manager
Pittsburgh Pirates

Other Sonflower Publishing Titles

The Big Brown Box
by Karen A. Bellamy

ISBN: 978-0-9713416-7-8
Category: Children Education

The Big Brown Box is a book written for Early Childhood—children in grades Kindergarten through 3rd grade. A book of poetry, The Big Brown Box depicts how the simple things are the pleasures of childhood.

The Big Brown Box is a story of how neighborhood children awaits a truck that commonly arrives to deliver items such as appliances, furniture, etc. to homes in their community and the fun and excitement that children have with the boxes after they are discarded.

The 24 page book is also accompanied with an audio (CD) narrated by the author.

Ephraim and the Bee
by Karen A. Bellamy

ISBN: 978-0-9887797-0-9
Category: Children Education
Price: $20.00

Ephraim and the Bee is an enlightening and illuminating children's story of a conversation and friendship that a boy has and makes with a bee while he is sitting and enjoying his lunch on a playground. Children are introduced to new words that will build their vocabulary. The book includes a CD narrated by the author.

Holding On
by Yolanda L. Chiestder

ISBN: 0-9713416-5-6
Category: Christian Education/ Devotional/ Women
Price: $14.99

Holding On is a book that will share the author's life experience coupled with biblical principles. It tells about her sheltered childhood, lonely teenage years, unsaved adult life, saved adult life, and her married (yet living as a single parent) life. It also shares the ups, downs, obstacles, and tragedies she faces, as she continues to persevere to the "Destiny" God has for her life.

Other Sonflower Publishing Titles

The LORD Gave Me A Song Too
by Herstine Wright

ISBN: 978-0-9887797-2-3
Category: Christian Education/Devotional songs
Paperback: 72 pages

The LORD Gave Me A Song Too is a revelation of the power and purpose of spiritual songs. It also includes a book of poetry/songs, an "Expression of the Heart."

A Report from The Heights
by Herstine Wright

ISBN: 978-0-9887797-1-6
Category: Christian Education/Devotiona
Paperback: 184 pages

A Report from The Heights is a Biblical teaching coupled with testimony of the hidden truths of **Seeing and Enjoying the Salvation of the LORD** daily. It is also a revelation of the **Attributes of the LORD'S Salvation** found in the Word of God and disclosed in His manifest Presence.

A Witness — The Spiritual Inheritance
by Herstine Wright

ISBN: 978-0-9887797-3-0
Category: Christian
Journal: 240 pages

This powerful journal is a recording of the believers' testimony of their relationship/communion/fellowship with the LORD on a daily basis.

Eyes Wide, Ears Wider
by Darrell "The Arkutec" Murray

ISBN: 978-0-9887797-4-7
Category: Poetry
Journal: 96 pages

Eyes Wide Ears Wider, The Thoughts of the Nights Air is vulnerability, desire, pain, inspiration, power, and victory in the form of poetry and short story. It dives deep into the realities of the heart, mind, and soul revealing strengths and insecurities that many of us battle with daily.

Other Sonflower Publishing Titles

YOU'RE WELCOME!
God's Expression of Gratitude
The Power of Giving Thanks
by Herstine Wright

ISBN: 978-0-9887797-5-4
Category: Christian Education/Devotional songs
Paperback: 134 pages

You're Welcome! God's Expression of Gratitude The Power of Giving Thanks is a powerful teaching, testimony, and revelation of the power of Giving Thanks to God. More importantly, it reveals God's RESPONSE to a grateful heart in the form of manifold blessings. *You're Welcome! God's Expression of Gratitude* also takes the believers to new levels and dimensions of praise and worship that will enable them to clearly hear the Voice of God.

www.ingramcontent.com/pod-product-compliance
Lightning Source LLC
Chambersburg PA
CBHW051947290426
44110CB00015B/2148